COURAGEOUS FAITH: EMBRACING GOD'S PURPOSE THROUGH LIFE'S GREATEST CHALLENGES

LOVE CHRISTOPHERS

CONTENTS

INTRODUCTION

The Call to Courageous Faith

This book is a journey of discovery—a journey into the heart of courageous faith. We will explore the profound connection between faith and courage, demonstrating how they are not merely complementary but intrinsically intertwined.

In this introductory chapter, we will begin by defining faith and courage within a biblical framework. We will examine what it truly means to trust in God and to act with courage, even when fear whispers doubts. We will delve into inspiring examples from Scripture, showcasing individuals who demonstrated unwavering faith in the face of adversity. Finally, we will recognize the courage that exists in the seemingly small, everyday moments of our lives, demonstrating that courageous faith is not reserved for the extraordinary but can be cultivated in the ordinary.

By the end of this chapter, you will have a deeper understanding of what courageous faith truly entails and how you can begin to cultivate it in your own life.

Life often demands more from us than we feel capable of giving. There are moments when shadows of doubt creep in, when the weight of the unknown seems paralyzing, and when fear whispers that we are alone in our struggles. Yet, it is in these very moments that courageous faith is born. Courageous faith acknowledges obstacles but trusts in a God greater than any challenge. It is an active decision to believe in His promises, even when the path ahead seems unclear. This faith invites us into a deeper reliance on God, transforming trials into testimonies and struggles into steps of victory. Through this book, you will explore what it means to live in the strength that comes from trusting God fully, discovering the unmatched freedom and joy found in a life rooted in unwavering faith. The purpose of this book is to inspire and empower you to embrace a faith so courageous that it transforms not only your life but also the lives of those around you, through insights from biblical heroes like Esther, David, and the Apostle Paul.

The purpose of this book is simple yet profound: to inspire and empower you to embrace a faith so courageous that it transforms not only your life but also the lives of those around you. This book aims to shed light on the relationship between faith and bravery, using insights from God's Word and personal experiences to inspire you to confront life's challenges with unwavering trust in His divine plan. From the biblical accounts of heroes like Esther, David, and the Apostle Paul to the everyday triumphs of modern believers, we will explore how faith enables courage to bloom in the face of adversity. Together, we will unpack how trusting in God unlocks the strength needed to face fears, overcome obstacles, and step into the fullness of His calling. This book serves as a guide and companion, supporting you as you boldly live for His glory, even in life's uncertainties.

A Journey of Faith and Courage

This book serves as a guiding light, providing a path through life's challenges with unwavering faith and unwavering courage. It is a passionate invitation to step beyond the boundaries of fear and into a life less ordinary—a life lived with bold conviction, even when adversity strikes. Through every chapter, we will explore the profound and inseparable connection between faith and courage, unveiling how these two pillars not only complement each other but are deeply intertwined.

Through the power of courageous faith, you will be equipped to confront your fears, identifying the hidden anxieties that have held you back from experiencing the abundant life God desires for you. You will learn to find peace in uncertainty, trusting fully in God's divine plan even when the road ahead is unclear. This book encourages you to boldly step into your unique God-given calling, overcoming obstacles with resilience and pursuing your purpose with passionate determination. Finally, it challenges you to live a life of impact, using your gifts and talents to inspire and transform the world around you, leaving behind a legacy of hope, love, and courage that glorifies Him.

This book is more than just a book to read; it's a journey to embrace, a challenge to surmount fear, and a step towards the fullness of faith. Its pages call out to the fearful yet hopeful heart, urging you to trust deeply, believe boldly, and embrace the extraordinary life God has prepared for you. Are you prepared to respond to the call of courageous faith? Let's embark on this journey together.

The Foundation of Courageous Faith

Courageous faith does not emerge in isolation; it is built upon a steady foundation of trust in God's character and His promises. To cultivate such faith, we must first know who God is—a faithful, unchanging, and sovereign Creator who holds all things together. It begins with understanding His heart for us, His love that pursues relentlessly, and His desire for us to walk confidently in the path He has prepared. Faith thrives when anchored in the truth of His Word and nurtured through intimate prayer, reflection, and communion with Him.

It entails opening our hearts to His guidance, even amidst uncertainty or overwhelming moments. Just as a tree's roots strengthen beneath the soil, our faith deepens when we allow God to speak into our lives, shaping us through the trials we face and the victories we celebrate.

Courageous faith also calls us to remember. When we reflect on how God has been faithful in the past—how He has carried us through storms and fulfilled His promises—we are reminded that He will do so again. These memories become markers of His goodness, enabling us to move forward boldly with the assurance that He is always with us. This unwavering trust in His faithfulness forms the foundation of courageous faith, enabling us to confront life's challenges with confidence and hope.

However, building this foundation requires intentionality. It requires us to open our hearts to His guidance, even when life feels uncertain or overwhelming. Faith is often nurtured in quiet, reflective moments when we seek His presence away from distractions. Just as a tree's roots strengthen beneath the soil, our faith deepens when we allow God to speak into our lives, shaping us through the trials we face and the victories we celebrate. *"But blessed is the one who trusts in the Lord, whose confidence is in him. They will resemble a tree that is water-planted and sends out roots along a stream. It does not fear when heat comes; its leaves are always green. In a year of drought, it remains unfazed and consistently produces fruit.* (Jeremiah 17:7-8).

Courageous faith also calls us to remember. When we reflect on how God has been faithful in the past—how He has carried us through storms and fulfilled His promises—we are reminded that He will do so again. *"Remember the wonders he has done, his miracles, and the judgments he pronounced"* (Psalm 105:5). These memories become markers of His goodness, enabling us to move forward boldly with the assurance that He is always with us. *"Be strong and courageous. Do not be afraid; do not be discouraged, for the Lord your God will be with you wherever you go"* (Joshua 1:9). This unwavering trust in His faithfulness forms the foundation of courageous faith, enabling us to confront life's challenges with confidence and hope.

Faith and Courage Go Hand in Hand

Faith provides the foundation for courage, enabling individuals to face fears confidently. Courage allows faith to manifest in action, leading to a transformative partnership.

In the journey of life, faith and courage work together to propel us towards our destinies. Faith gives courage its foundation, while courage allows faith to manifest in action. James 2:26 reminds us, *"Faith without works is dead."* Courageous actions give life to the faith we profess.

Consider the story of Joshua, who was called to lead the Israelites into the Promised Land after Moses' death. God's words to him were clear: *"Be strong and courageous. Do not be afraid; do not be discouraged, for the Lord your God will be with you wherever you go"* (Joshua 1:9). Joshua's courage was rooted in his faith in God's promise and presence. Likewise, your courage can flourish when you trust that God is with you, guiding and strengthening you every step of the way.

True faith is not blind optimism; it's a courageous leap into the unknown, a steadfast reliance on a power greater than ourselves. Hebrews 11:1 defines faith as *"the assurance of things hoped for, the conviction of things not seen."* This powerful verse highlights the courageous act of believing in something unseen, trusting in God's promises even when circumstances seem bleak.

In 2 Timothy 1:7, Paul reminds us that *"God has not given us a spirit of fear, but of power and of love and of self-control."* Courage is not just a human trait but a divine gift, a manifestation of God's grace that empowers us to confront challenges with unwavering resolve.

Faith and courage are inseparable because faith provides the foundation for courage. When we truly believe in God's love and sovereignty, we are empowered to face our fears confidently.

Imagine a sturdy house built on a shaky foundation. The slightest tremor could cause it to crumble. Similarly, courage without faith is like a building without a solid base—easily shaken by fear and doubt.

True faith, however, provides an unshakable foundation. It's akin to constructing on solid, unwavering ground. When we believe in God's unwavering love and His sovereign plan for our lives, we are no longer tethered to our own limited perspectives or paralyzed by fear.

"The Lord is my light and my salvation—whom shall I fear? The Lord is the stronghold of my life—of whom shall I be afraid?" (Psalm 27:1) This powerful psalm expresses the profound peace that comes from trusting in God's unwavering presence and protection. Fear loses its grip when we acknowledge God as our refuge, our strength, and our source of security. We are empowered to face challenges with courage, knowing that God is with us every step of the way.

Furthermore, courage fuels our faith. Taking courageous steps even when we are uncertain deepens our trust in God and strengthens our reliance on His guidance.

When we step out in faith, even when fear whispers doubts, we are demonstrating our trust in God's promises. We are saying, "I believe in you, God. I trust that you will guide my steps and provide for my needs." Each courageous act, whether it's forgiving someone who has wronged us, sharing our faith with others, or pursuing a seemingly impossible dream, strengthens our faith and deepens our relationship with God.

Through these experiences, we begin to see firsthand God's faithfulness. We witness His provision, experience His comfort, and encounter His guidance in unexpected ways. These encounters strengthen our faith and motivate us to make even more significant strides in faith.

God's Word and Spirit empower us to live boldly, trusting His promises and confidently walking in His plans.

The Bible is filled with promises of God's unwavering love, protection, and guidance. As we immerse ourselves in Scripture, these promises become a source of strength and encouragement. They equip us to face life's challenges with courage and confidence, knowing that God is always with us.

He gives us the strength, wisdom, and discernment we need to navigate life's complexities and fulfill our God-given purposes. He empowers us to overcome fear, resist temptation, and live lives that reflect God's love and grace.

By embracing the power of the Holy Spirit and living in accordance with God's Word, we can cultivate a life of courageous faith. We can face our fears, overcome obstacles, and confidently pursue our dreams, knowing that God is our strength and our refuge.

When faith and courage converge, they produce a life of purpose and transformation. This partnership compels us to step out of our comfort zones and into the extraordinary plans God has prepared for us. It is in these moments of bravery, rooted in unwavering trust, that we experience the fullness of His power and love. Courageous faith is not content with passivity; it calls us to action, to be instruments of hope and change in the world around us.

Consider the example of Peter stepping out of the boat to walk on water toward Jesus (Matthew 14:28–33). His faith motivated him to take that first bold step, and his courage kept him moving forward in the midst of uncertainty. While his focus wavered for a moment, leading to fear and doubt, the hand of Jesus was there to steady him. This story reminds us that faith and courage are not about perfection—they are about trusting God to meet us where we are, even when we falter, and helping us to rise again.

Living by faith and courage involves boldly facing struggles and fears with the unwavering assurance that God is by our side, guiding us through every challenge. Romans 8:31 reminds us, *"If God is for us, who can be against us?"* This truth empowers us to overcome obstacles and partner with Him in fulfilling His purposes. Every act of faith, no matter how small, becomes a declaration of His strength and a testament to His faithfulness.

Ultimately, courageous faith transforms how we see the world and our place in it. It enables us to see challenges as opportunities for growth and trials as pathways to deeper reliance on God. It inspires us to celebrate His victories and to trust His redemptive work in all things. Through this perspective, we start to live boldly, not for ourselves but as mirrors of His glory, spreading His love and light to a world in need. A life lived abundantly in His presence is undoubtedly one that exhibits faith and courage.

A Personal Story/Testimony

I'll never forget a season in my life when fear and uncertainty seemed to overshadow everything. It was a time when my carefully constructed plans unraveled, leaving me in a place of deep vulnerability. I was facing the collapse of a major project that I had poured my heart into, a loss that hit both professionally and personally. At the same time, the burden of fractured relationships added another layer of pain that

I wasn't sure how to mend. I felt exposed—without answers, without direction, and without strength.

One particularly hard evening, with a heart full of questions, I cried out to God, not even knowing what I was asking for. In that silence, I was drawn to Proverbs 3:5–6, a passage I had known for years but never truly clung to before. "Trust in the Lord with all your heart and lean not on your own understanding; in all your ways submit to him, and he will make your paths straight." For the first time, I saw in those words a gentle invitation to release control—not to figure everything out, but to simply trust.

It didn't happen overnight, but little by little, God began to renew me. He brought clarity where there had been confusion, peace where there had been turmoil, and the courage to take small steps at a time. That season taught me one of the most profound lessons of my life—that faith isn't about having all the answers but about following the One who does.

This book is built upon stories like that—honest moments of despair that are transformed into hope through faith. As you read, my hope is that you will find reflections of your own story and be reassured that you are never alone in your struggles. The same God who was faithful to carry me will be faithful to carry you, too.

Encouragement to Begin the Journey

This book accompanies you on the journey to courageous faith. If you're encountering challenges in your family, career, or personal relationship with God, the principles in this book aim to uplift and guide you. You are not alone in your struggles, and you are certainly not powerless. As you read, let the stories of biblical heroes inspire you, let the promises of Scripture strengthen you, and let the testimonies of others remind you of what is possible when faith meets courage.

Now is the moment for you to rise, stand firm, and advance with unwavering faith. "But those who hope in the Lord will renew their strength. They will soar on wings like eagles; they will run and not grow weary; they will walk and not be faint" (Isaiah 40:31).

Walking Through the Valleys

Faith is often forged most deeply in the valleys of life—the spaces where shadows linger, questions arise, and answers may seem painfully out of reach. In these moments, when everything around us feels uncertain, God invites us to draw closer. Valleys do not signify abandonment but serve as reminders that even in the darkness, His presence remains constant.

Consider the story of David, a man who knew both the heights of triumph and the depths of despair. When he penned Psalm 23, "Even though I walk through the darkest valley, I will fear no evil, for you are with me," he was not writing from a place of ease or comfort. He was speaking from experience—words born from hardship and struggle. David understood that trust in God does not eliminate the valleys but transforms how we walk through them.

The valleys in our lives test and strengthen our faith in ways the mountaintops never could. They strip away distractions and bring clarity to what really matters. They teach us reliance, deepen our trust, and remind us that the journey isn't about our strength but about His. As daunting as the valleys may seem, each one carries the potential for profound growth, renewal, and intimacy with God.

If you are currently facing challenges, take heart and find strength in knowing that you are not alone. Your story isn't over. The same God who walked with David is walking with you, too. And just as valleys are part of the landscape of life, so too are the peaks that follow them. Continue to trust, press on, and remember that even in the midst of challenges, His faithfulness remains unwavering, guiding you through every trial.

The Power of Surrender

Surrender is one of the most profound and yet most challenging acts of faith. It requires us to lay down our plans, our fears, and our desires at the feet of the One who knows all, sees all, and holds all in His hands. To surrender is to acknowledge that we don't have all the answers—and we don't need to—because we serve a God who does. But in a world that prizes control and independence, the act of surrender can feel counterintuitive, even impossible.

When we think of surrender, it's natural to associate it with loss or defeat. Yet, in God's kingdom, surrender is the beginning of victory. Consider the life of Jesus, who, in the garden of Gethsemane, prayed with a heart of anguish, "Not my will, but yours be done" (Luke 22:42). His surrender led to the most triumphant act of redemption the world has ever known. Through surrendering His will to the Father, Jesus showed us that true strength lies in yielding, and true victory comes through obedience.

Surrender doesn't mean giving up; it means giving over. It's an intentional act of trust, relinquishing control in exchange for God's wisdom and guidance. It's a declaration that His ways are higher than ours (Isaiah 55:8–9) and an invitation for Him to work in and through us in ways we could never imagine. While surrender may not bring about immediate relief, it does result in profound peace because it comes from knowing that a loving and omnipotent God is holding you securely.

If you're struggling with surrender today, remember that it's a journey, not a one-time decision. It's natural to feel hesitant, ask questions, and grapple with what it means to trust fully. God isn't asking for perfection; He's asking for a willing heart. And as you take each step of faith, no matter how small, you'll begin to experience the freedom and joy that only surrender can bring. Surrender aligns our hearts with God's purpose, revealing the abundant life He has prepared for us.

Are you ready to embark on this journey of discovery?

This book invites you to embrace a life of courage, grounded in unwavering faith in God. It's a call to step out of your comfort zone, to embrace the unknown, and to live a life of purpose and impact.

Are you prepared to respond to the call of courageous faith?

Let's embark on this journey together.

Disclaimer: This chapter provides general information and is not intended as a substitute for professional counseling or therapy. If you are struggling with anxiety or fear, please consult with a qualified mental health professional.

Note: This information is for general knowledge and informational purposes only. For medical advice or diagnosis, consult a professional.

Part I: Understanding Courageous Faith

CHAPTER I

WHAT IS COURAGEOUS FAITH?

Faith and courage are two powerful forces that, when combined, enable us to live boldly and victoriously for God. Courageous faith goes beyond simply believing in God; it is a deep trust that motivates us to obey, particularly when faced with uncertainty. It is the willingness to say "yes" to God, no matter the cost, because we know He is faithful to fulfill His promises. This kind of faith empowers us to face trials with confidence, knowing that our strength comes not from ourselves but from the One who holds all things in His hands. It dares us to venture beyond our comfort zones and wholeheartedly embrace His plan, even when the results are unknown. True courageous faith pushes us to rely wholly on God's sovereignty and walk in the purpose He has laid out for us.

What does it mean to live a life of courageous faith? For many, faith is seen as a quiet belief—a private trust in God's power and goodness. But when paired with courage, faith transforms into something bold, active, and unshakable. Courageous faith compels us not only to believe but to act, stepping forward into the unknown because we trust in the One who holds the future.

Courageous faith does not mean being without fear. Instead, it involves finding strength during times of fear, trusting that God's promises outweigh our uncertainties. It inspires us to stand up, relinquish our plans, and embrace God's call, even when it pushes us beyond our comfort zones.

We'll find inspiration in stories of those who trusted God despite overwhelming odds and uncover how small, everyday acts of courage can be foundational to a life of faith. Together, we'll also reflect on the powerful act of surrender—letting go of our own control and placing our trust in a God who is greater than ourselves.

Through courageous faith, we can experience a deeper relationship with God and uncover the purpose He has for each of us. So let's dive into this journey together and discover what it truly means to live a life of courageous faith. Let's embrace the unknown with confidence, trusting that God is always by our side, guiding us with His love and strength. And let's remember that true courage comes not from ourselves but from the One who created us and equips us with everything we need to face whatever challenges come our way.

Defining Faith and Courage in a Biblical Context

This book is an invitation to embrace a courageous life rooted in unwavering faith in God. But what exactly does "courageous faith" mean? Defining Faith and Courage in a Biblical Context

Defining Faith and Courage in a Biblical Context

This book invites readers to embrace a courageous life rooted in unwavering faith in God. But what exactly does "courageous faith" mean?

- **Faith:** In a biblical context, faith is more than just believing in God's existence. It's a **deep and abiding trust in God's character, His promises, and His sovereignty.** Hebrews 11:1 defines faith as "the assurance of things hoped for, the conviction of things not seen." It's a confident reliance on God's invisible hand, even when circumstances seem uncertain or bleak. Faith is believing with certainty in things we cannot see, trusting that God is true to His word and will fulfill His promises. Hebrews 11:1 defines faith as *"the substance of things hoped for, the evidence of things not seen."* Faith is not passive; it is alive and active, requiring us to trust God beyond our understanding. It involves confident reliance on God's invisible hand, even when circumstances seem uncertain or bleak, because faith believes in what we cannot see.

- **Courage** is not the absence of fear but the ability to act despite being afraid. It's the strength to courageously confront challenges, conquer obstacles, and relentlessly pursue your God-given purpose, even when the path ahead is shrouded in uncertainty and the risks loom large. Biblical courage comes from knowing that God is with us and for us. As Paul writes in 2 Timothy 1:7, *"For God has not given us a spirit of fear, but of power and of love and of a sound mind."* Courage is the inner strength to follow God's commands, even in challenging situations or when faced with resistance. The English word "courage" comes from the Latin word cor, which means heart. Throughout the Bible, courage is often associated with having a strong heart or being of good courage (Joshua 1:9). Courage is not the absence of fear but rather the ability to take action despite our fears. It takes strength and determination to stand firm in our faith even when we face challenges or uncertain circumstances. And as followers of Christ, our courage ultimately comes from Him, for He has overcome the world (John 16:33).

In essence, courageous faith embodies a fusion of trust, obedience, and unwavering determination. It is choosing to believe in God's promises, acting on that belief with boldness, and persevering through all circumstances by His strength.

Notable biblical figures who have displayed courageous faith include Abraham, Moses, Joshua, Esther, David, Shadrach, Meshach, and Abednego.

We find numerous instances of men and women who bravely trusted in God despite overwhelming odds throughout the Bible. Some notable examples include:

- Abraham leaving his homeland to follow God's call (Genesis 12:1-4)
- Moses confronting Pharaoh to free the Israelites from slavery (Exodus 5-14)
- Joshua leading the Israelites into the Promised Land (Joshua 1)
- Esther risking her life to save her people (Esther 4-9)
- David facing Goliath with only a slingshot and five stones (1 Samuel 17)

- Shadrach, Meshach, and Abednego refusing to bow down to King Nebuchadnezzar's idol (Daniel 3)

These individuals exemplified courageous faith by faithfully following God's directives amidst adversity and demonstrating unwavering trust in His sovereignty over their situations. They faced seemingly impossible situations, yet they stood firm in their beliefs because of their unwavering trust in God.

Other Examples from Scripture

The Bible is filled with stories of men and women who displayed courageous faith. These individuals were not without flaws or fears, yet they chose to trust God and step into the unknown.

1. **Abraham—Trusting God's Promise**

Abraham's life is a profound example of courageous faith. When God called him to leave his homeland and go to a place He would show him, Abraham obeyed without knowing the destination (Genesis 12:1-4). Later, he displayed extraordinary faith when God tested him by asking him to sacrifice his son, Isaac. Abraham's willingness to obey, even in this heart-wrenching command, demonstrated his unwavering trust in God's provision (Genesis 22:1-14). This act of faith, which was subject to numerous trials and tests, stands as a potent example of how obedience can transform.

1. **Esther—Risking Everything to Save Others**

Queen Esther's story reminds us that courage often means standing up for others. When her people were threatened with annihilation, Esther risked her life by approaching the king without being summoned—a move that could have resulted in her death. Her declaration, “If I perish, I perish.” (Esther 4:16), exemplifies the kind of boldness that flows from faith in God’s plan and providence. Her act of bravery saved her people and is a powerful reminder that even one person can make a significant difference.

1. **Paul—Persevering Through Trials**

Unwavering courage and faith were hallmarks of the apostle Paul's ministry. Despite facing imprisonment, beatings, shipwrecks, and constant danger, Paul continued to proclaim the gospel with unwavering courage and conviction (Acts 14:19-20). In 2 Corinthians 12:9-10, he writes, “But He said to me, ‘My grace is sufficient for you, for my power is made perfect in weakness.’ Therefore I will boast all the more gladly about my weaknesses, so that Christ’s power may rest on me.” Paul's life shows that courageous faith empowers us to endure and triumph through hardships. His life serves as a powerful testament to the enduring power of faith in the face of adversity.

These biblical figures, and countless others, demonstrate that courageous faith is not a passive state of being. It's a dynamic force that compels us to action, to step out in obedience to God's calling, even when the path ahead is uncertain and the risks seem overwhelming.

Recognizing the Small Moments of Bravery in Everyday Life

Exploring how acts of bravery in everyday life, such as forgiveness, standing up for righteousness, and trusting God in uncertainties, reflect a heart inclined towards reliance on Him. Courageous faith is not reserved for monumental events; it is often revealed in the small, quiet moments of daily life. It might look like offering forgiveness when it feels undeserved, standing up for what is right in a challenging situation, or simply trusting God through the uncertainties of an ordinary day. Acts of bravery can include choosing to be patient instead of getting frustrated, showing kindness instead of anger, or holding onto faith rather than succumbing to fear.

These seemingly small decisions reflect a heart that is postured toward relying on God. These seemingly small decisions reflect a heart that is postured toward relying on God. Just as David trusted in God's providence as a shepherd long before facing Goliath, our everyday choices to trust God prepare us for greater acts of faithfulness. Moments of daily courage, though they may go unnoticed by others, are invaluable to our spiritual growth and bring us closer to living a life fully dependent on God's strength.

- **Choosing Integrity:** It takes courage to maintain integrity in a world that often celebrates shortcuts and compromises. Choosing honesty, even when it might cost an opportunity or lead to inconvenience, is a bold act of faith. For instance, refusing to exaggerate achievements on a resume or turning down an unethical proposition demonstrates a reliance on God's provision rather than worldly schemes. For instance, refusing to exaggerate achievements on a resume or turning down an unethical proposition demonstrates a reliance on God's provision rather than worldly schemes. These decisions, though difficult, affirm a commitment to align with God's character. Integrity not only honors God but also builds a foundation of trust and authenticity in our relationships and daily interactions. Integrity not only honors God but also builds a foundation of trust and authenticity in our relationships and daily interactions. By choosing what is right over what is easy, we reflect a deep trust in God's plan and His ability to meet our needs in His perfect timing.

- **Facing Personal Fears:** Confronting personal fears like public speaking, initiating difficult conversations, or pursuing a new career path showcases courageous faith in action, trusting God's guidance in the face of uncertainty. Facing personal fears requires trusting that God will provide the strength and direction needed to move forward. It's in these moments of uncertainty and vulnerability that we can witness God's power working through our weaknesses. Every small step of faith provides us with the chance to rely on God's promises and advance in our spiritual development. When we confidently move into unfamiliar territory guided by His wisdom, His grace works within us to turn our fears into a testament of His unfailing faithfulness.

- **Extending Grace and Forgiveness:** Forgiving someone who has wronged you is a profound act of courageous faith. It requires setting aside bitterness and surrendering your pain to God, trusting Him to bring justice and healing in His perfect time. Grace and forgiveness reflect the love God has shown us through Christ, reminding us that we, too, are recipients of unmerited mercy. It is not an easy path, but it is a powerful way to release the burden of resentment and invite God's peace into our hearts. By forgiving others, we show obedience to His command and create space for reconciliation and restoration in relationships, demonstrating the transforming power of His love.

- **Choosing forgiveness over bitterness:** Choosing forgiveness over bitterness is an act of courage that releases the grip of resentment and allows God's healing and restoration to flow into relationships. Bitterness may feel like a natural response to pain, but it often leads to deeper emotional and spiritual wounds. Forgiveness, on the other hand, allows us to break free from the chains of negativity that can weigh down our hearts. It does not mean that the hurt is forgotten or that the wrong is justified; rather, it is a conscious decision to relinquish anger and trust God's justice. Through forgiveness, we open ourselves to healing and align our hearts with God's will, experiencing the profound freedom that comes from walking in His grace.

- **Stepping outside your comfort zone:** Taking bold actions that push you beyond your usual boundaries is a powerful display of courageous faith that can bring you nearer to God's intended path for you. Trying something new, whether it's pursuing a calling you've felt hesitant about or taking on a challenge that stretches your abilities, demonstrates trust in God's plan. Sharing your faith with someone, especially when it feels intimidating, can instill seeds of hope and truth in their life, reflecting God's love and grace. When we step out in faith, we open ourselves to new opportunities for growth and witness the power of God's strength working in our weaknesses.

- **Overcoming temptation:** Resisting the urge to gossip, choosing healthy habits over instant gratification, and prioritizing prayer and meditation amidst the chaos of daily life are small victories that build resilience and strengthen character. These intentional choices, though seemingly small, reflect a heart committed to living in alignment with God's will. By turning away from negative tendencies like gossip, we cultivate kindness and integrity, fostering relationships rooted in love and understanding.

Opting for healthy habits equips us to honor our bodies as temples of the Holy Spirit, reinforcing self-discipline and stewardship over the blessings we've been given. Prioritizing prayer and meditation creates a sacred space to seek God's guidance and peace, anchoring us in His presence even during life's storms. Together, these actions form a foundation of spiritual growth, keeping us grounded and prepared to face challenges with unwavering faith.

Even the smallest acts of bravery honor God and build spiritual resilience. Matthew 25:21 reminds us of the reward for faithfulness in small things: "Well done, good and faithful servant! You have been faithful with a few things; I will put you in charge of many things." These words echo the truth that each step of faith, no matter how modest, is deeply significant to God. They reassure us that He sees and values our efforts to obey and trust Him, even in the face of fear or uncertainty.

This book is an invitation to cultivate a life of courageous faith—a life characterized by unwavering trust in God and the courage to live out that trust in every aspect of your life. It urges us to take bold steps forward, confident that He goes before us and equips us for every good work. Together, we will delve into the essence of living boldly for Christ, discovering joy and purpose in each obedient step we take with Him.

The Power of Surrender in Courageous Faith

At the core of courageous faith lies surrender—letting go of our own plans and trusting in God's perfect will for our lives. Surrendering our desires and yielding to God's guidance demands humility and trust. Yet, this surrender is where we find true strength and courage, for it is in our weakness that He shows His power (2 Corinthians

12:9). Surrendering to God is not about abandoning responsibility but about acknowledging that His ways are higher than ours and trusting His perfect timing and provision.

When we release our grip on control and place our lives in His hands, we are met with a peace that transcends understanding (Philippians 4:7). This peace comes from knowing that God is faithful and that He cares for every detail of our lives. As we surrender to Him and trust in His goodness, we can have confidence that He will equip us with everything we need to face whatever challenges come our way. As we surrender to Him and trust in His goodness, we can have confidence that He will equip us with everything we need to face whatever challenges come our way. When we surrender to God, we gain access to His power, which empowers us to live fearlessly, love profoundly, and achieve His purpose for our lives.

In a world that often glorifies self-sufficiency and independence, surrender may seem like weakness. But in reality, it takes great strength to let go of our own plans and trust in God's plan for us. Surrendering is an act of bravery that requires courage and faith in the One who holds all things together (Colossians 1:17). As we surrender, we align ourselves with His perfect will, walking confidently in the path He has set before us. This surrender is not a one-time event but a daily choice to lay down our own desires and embrace God's plans for our lives.

Through surrender, we find freedom from the weight of trying to control every aspect of our lives. We can let go of the pressure to always have it all together and trust that God is in control. We are not meant to carry the weight of the world on our shoulders but rather to surrender it to the One who has already overcome it (John 16:33). Letting go and trusting in His plan allows us to experience true peace and rest, knowing that He is working all things together for our good (Romans 8:28).

In our ongoing journey towards courageous faith, let us always recall the significance of surrender and unwavering trust in God's perfect will for our lives. May we daily choose to lay down our own plans and embrace His, knowing that He is faithful and good. Through surrender, we find the strength and courage to live boldly for Christ, trusting in His power and provision every step of the way. So let us continue to cultivate a heart of surrender, as it is through this act of faith that we can truly experience the fullness of God's love and purpose for our lives. Let us choose courageous faith over fear, knowing that through Him we can do all things (Philippians 4:13). The journey may not always be easy, but with surrendered hearts and unwavering faith, we can overcome every obstacle and fulfill our divine calling.

Continuing the Journey of Courageous Faith

As we continue to grow in our understanding and practice of courageous faith, let us remember that it is a **process, not a destination.** Faith is a journey of constant learning, trusting, and growing. Along the way, we will face trials, challenges, and even moments of doubt, but these are opportunities for God to strengthen us and reveal His power through our lives.

Courageous faith is not about having all the answers or being fearless—it is about trusting the One who does. It is about stepping forward in obedience, even when the path ahead is unclear, and finding peace in knowing that God is always with us. As we continue this journey, we are reminded of the words in Philippians 1:6:

"Being confident of this, that He who began a good work in you will carry it on to completion until the day of Christ Jesus."

Holding Fast to Faith

Life's struggles are inevitable, but our faith equips us to face them with courage and perseverance. Trusting in His character and sovereignty gives us the confidence to navigate life's uncertainties and proclaim His goodness to those around us.

Courageous faith allows us to:

- Stand firm in trials, knowing that God is our anchor (Hebrews 6:19).
- Surrender our fears, trusting in His perfect love (1 John 4:18).
- Live boldly for His glory, reflecting His love and hope to the world (Matthew 5:16).

Opening Our Hearts to Transformation

Faith combined with courage is transformative. It shapes our character, deepens our trust in God, and empowers us to impact the lives of others. Every act of courageous faith—whether small or monumental—becomes a testimony of God's power and love.

As we journey together, let's open our hearts and minds to God's lessons. Let's allow Him to mold us into people who reflect His love, mercy, and strength in everything we do.

Jesus said in John 10:10:

"I have come that they may have life, and have it to the full."

A life of courageous faith is a life lived in the fullness of God's purpose and abundance.

Embracing Courageous Faith

Biblical figures and ordinary individuals alike exemplify courageous faith as a potent force that empowers us to conquer obstacles and align with God's divine purpose for our lives. Taking action, trusting in His provision, embracing integrity, facing personal fears, extending grace and forgiveness, and stepping outside our comfort zones all require courage. But as we continue on this journey of courageous faith, we can rest assured that His grace is sufficient for us and His power is made perfect in our weaknesses. Let us boldly embrace this dynamic force of

Each of these acts—trying something new, sharing your faith with someone you know, or speaking up for what you believe in—are powerful expressions of courageous faith. They require us to place our trust in God and step into the unknown, even when fear tries to hold us back. Trying something new allows God to work through us in unexpected ways, reminding us that His strength is made perfect in our weakness. Sharing your faith, whether with a friend or loved one, can be a transformational experience that not only blesses them but deepens your own relationship with God. Speaking up for what you believe in, especially in challenging situations, is a bold testament to God's truth and light, showing others the unwavering power of faith in action.

Encouragement to Cultivate Courageous Faith

Courageous faith urges us to purposefully and boldly live for God, particularly when faced with uncertainty or challenges. It teaches us to rely not on our own understanding or strength but on His unshakeable promises. Every act of obedience transforms into a form of worship, showcasing our reliance on His flawless design. Every moment of courageous faith, whether it involves venturing into unfamiliar territory, forgiving someone who has wronged us, or standing firm in our convictions despite opposition, serves as an opportunity to shine His light in a world that is broken. This faith not only changes our inner being but also motivates others to pursue the same hope and confidence discovered in Him.

With each leap of faith, we discover anew the depth of His love, the certainty of His presence, and the power of His grace to sustain us. May we move forward with confidence, knowing that God, who never fails us, is with us. May we be a light in the darkness, sharing His love and truth with all those around us. May we be a light in the darkness, sharing His love and truth with all those around us. And may our surrendered hearts be a constant reminder that it is through Him alone that we can do all things, for He is our strength and salvation. So let us walk confidently, knowing that as we surrender to God, He will lead us towards a life of courage, hope, and fulfillment that brings glory to His name. So let us continue to cultivate courageous faith each day, trusting in God's perfect plan and purpose for our lives. Let us

Courageous faith is a journey that progresses gradually, not an immediate destination. Each decision to trust God, whether in the extraordinary challenges or the simple moments of daily life, builds a foundation of unwavering faith.

As you consider the stories of Abraham, Esther, and Paul and even reflect on your own life, take heart in this truth: God equips those He calls. He does not demand perfection but asks for a heart willing to say, *"Here I am, Lord. Send me"* (Isaiah 6:8). Your availability, not your ability, makes God's power evident.

Take comfort in knowing that the same God who parted the sea for Moses, emboldened Esther before the king, and transformed Paul is present with you today. His promises are unfailing, and His Spirit within you remains a steadfast source of strength, guidance, and hope.

Let us hold onto the promise declared in Joshua 1:9: *"Have I not commanded you? Be strong and courageous. Do not be afraid; do not be discouraged, for the Lord your God will be with you wherever you go."* This verse is not just a reminder but a call to action—to walk boldly in faith, knowing you are never alone. Embarking on the journey of courageous faith starts with a single step forward.

Embarking on the journey of courageous faith starts with a single step forward. Will you choose to entrust your faith in Him today and take that initial step of trust?

CHAPTER 2

FEAR AND FAITH: A BALANCING ACT

On one hand, fear warns us of potential dangers and uncertainties, while on the other, faith calls us to trust in God's promises and obey. Balancing fear and faith involves letting faith guide our actions instead of letting fear control them, rather than trying to eliminate fear altogether.

Fear is a primal emotion, like a persistent whisper of doubt that can paralyze even the most determined soul. For example, Moses felt hesitation when called by God (Exodus 4:10). It's like a cold, paralyzing grip of anxiety that takes away joy and crushes dreams. Yet fear is not the enemy. It's a natural human response to uncertainty and danger. Acknowledging fear's presence is the first crucial step in overcoming it.

On the other hand, faith acts as the remedy for fear, providing a strong belief in God's promises to counter the uncertainties caused by fear. It is the steady assurance that God is in control, even in the face of life's unknowns. Faith does not deny the existence of challenges; instead, it empowers us to confront them with courage and trust. Choosing faith involves acknowledging that even though we may not see everything clearly, we trust in a God who does. Faith gives us the unwavering strength and courage to venture into the unknown, defying fear's grip that tries to impede our advancement. Together, fear and faith can coexist, with faith taking the lead as we learn to lean on God's guidance and promises.

But how do we cultivate this delicate balance between fear and faith? It starts with surrender.

- **Surrendering our fears to God** doesn't mean ignoring or suppressing them. It means acknowledging them honestly, naming them, and then intentionally releasing them to God. We entrust our anxieties to His care, knowing that He is bigger than any fear we may face.
    - **Practical Tip:** Spend time in prayer, specifically naming your fears and anxieties. Ask God to replace these fears with His peace and to guide you with His wisdom.
- **Surrendering our plans and desires to His will** doesn't mean we become passive or complacent. It means aligning our desires with God's will and seeking His guidance in all our decisions. We must be willing to let go of our own agendas and embrace His plan, even if it differs from what we envisioned.
    - **Practical Tip:** Spend time in prayer and scripture study, seeking God's guidance in your life choices. Be open to unexpected opportunities and willing to adjust your plans as needed.
- **Choosing to trust in His ways even when they may not align with our vision:** Trusting God requires us to

believe that His ways are always higher than our ways and His thoughts are higher than our thoughts (Isaiah 55:9). This means trusting His timing, accepting His will, and finding peace in the unknown.

- **Practical Tip:** Practice gratitude for the blessings in your life, even during challenging times. Focus on God's faithfulness in the past and trust that He will continue to be faithful in the future.

Cultivating this balance between fear and faith is an ongoing process. It requires consistent effort, intentional practice, and a willingness to surrender our own will to God's. However, the rewards of this surrender are immeasurable. We experience a peace that transcends all understanding as we learn to trust in God's perfect plan and embrace His guidance.

As we surrender, we must also actively choose to immerse ourselves in God's truth, deliberately shifting our focus from fear to the promises and assurances found in His word. It involves intentionally immersing your mind in God's promises from Scripture, redirecting your focus from worldly concerns to the truths that provide strength and assurance in times of fear. It means spending time in prayer, seeking His wisdom and guidance as we face our fears. It also means surrounding ourselves with a community of believers who can encourage and support us in our journey of faith.

Choosing to live with courageous faith, despite its challenges, is worthwhile because it leads to a life brimming with purpose, resilience, and a profound connection with God. It allows us to experience the fullness of God's love and purpose for our lives. As we continue to surrender our fears and trust in Him, He will guide us towards a life that overflows with courage, hope, and joy. Therefore, let us embrace the delicate balance between fear and faith, confident that by relying on God's strength, we can conquer any challenge that may arise. Let us choose courageous faith every day, trusting in the One who has already overcome the world. So may our lives be a testament to His power and love as we walk fearlessly in His grace and truth. And may we never forget that with God by our side, there is nothing that we cannot conquer through faith. Let us continue to strive towards a life of courageous faith, knowing that it is not just for ourselves but also for the glory of our faithful Father in heaven.

Understanding Fear as a Natural Emotion

Fear is a natural and instinctive response to perceived threats or uncertainties. It is a mechanism that God designed to protect us, alert us to danger, and prompt caution. Even biblical heroes experienced fear. Moses hesitated when God called him to lead Israel, citing his lack of eloquence (Exodus 4:10). Gideon doubted his ability to deliver Israel from the Midianites, questioning God's choice of him as a leader (Judges 6:15).

While fear itself is not sinful, allowing it to control our actions can hinder us from fulfilling God's plans. Fear becomes troublesome when it immobilizes us, prompts disobedience, or weakens our trust in God. Instead of being enslaved by fear, we are called to confront it with faith. Faith transforms fear, reminding us that God is greater than any obstacle or uncertainty we face. Faith empowers us to move forward with courage, trusting in His perfect plan and timing.

Living with Courageous Faith

Living with courageous faith is not a one-time event but a daily choice to trust in God and His promises. It requires vulnerability, humility, and surrender of our fears to Him. Additionally, it calls us to take action and step out in faith even when it feels uncomfortable or uncertain.

When we choose to live with courageous faith, we are not promised an easy journey. In fact, Jesus Himself warned that following Him would involve challenges (John 16:33). But He also reassured us that through Him, we are empowered to overcome fear and face any obstacle with courage (1 John 4:4). Our faith is not rooted in our own strength or abilities, but in the unchanging nature of our faithful God.

Conclusion

Fear and faith will always coexist, but it is our choice which one we let guide our lives. As we continue to cultivate courageous faith each day, may we remember that it is not about eliminating fear but rather trusting in God's perfect plan and purpose for our lives. Let us embrace both fear and faith, letting faith lead the way as we press on towards a life of courage and fulfillment in Him. Let us choose to live with courageous faith every day and witness the ways God transforms our fears into stepping stones towards His greater plans for us. So let us hold fast to His promises, trusting in His unchanging love and power, and live boldly for His glory. May our lives be a testament to the beautiful balance of fear and faith, where God's perfect love casts out all fear (1 John 4:18) and empowers us to walk confidently through whatever challenges may come. Let us continue to choose faith over fear and watch as God works wonders in our lives.

Keep moving forward with courageous faith. Your journey is just beginning. So let your heart be filled with hope, your steps guided by trust, and your spirit strengthened by His grace. For you serve a God who is bigger than any fear you face and who will never leave you nor forsake you (Deuteronomy 31:6). Hold on to His promises, surrender your fears, and live each day with courageous faith. The best is still to come. Therefore, let us persist in maintaining a balance between fear and faith, trusting in the goodness of God's plans and the unwavering love of God. May it be said of us as it was said of Abraham, "He did not waver through unbelief regarding the promise of God but was strengthened in his faith and gave glory to God" (Romans 4:20 NIV). Let our lives be a reflection of fearless faith lived out for Him. Amen.

Biblical Reassurance: "Fear Not, For I Am With You"

Throughout Scripture, God repeatedly tells His people, "Fear not." This divine reassurance is not an empty command; it is always accompanied by the promise of His presence and power.

- **Isaiah 41:10 reminds** us, "Fear not, for I am with you; do not be dismayed, for I am your God. I will strengthen you and help you; I will uphold you with my righteous right hand." This verse highlights that God's constant presence is the ultimate antidote to fear. By turning our focus from our own weaknesses to His boundless strength, fear loses its power over us.

- Similarly, Psalm 23:4 declares, "Even though I walk through the darkest valley, I will fear no evil, for you are with me; your rod and your staff, they comfort me." David's unwavering confidence in God's protection and guidance empowered him to endure the most challenging trials without giving in to fear. His reliance on God's presence serves as a timeless example of faith in action.

- **John 14:27**: Lastly, in John 14:27, Jesus offers profound comfort to His disciples, saying, "Peace I leave with you; my peace I give you. I do not give to you as the world gives. Do not let your hearts be troubled, and do not be afraid." The peace bestowed by Jesus transcends worldly offerings, calming our hearts and equipping us with the courage to confront any challenge.

These passages remind us that God's promises are not only meant to quell our fears but also to strengthen our faith. His presence, peace, and power provide an unwavering foundation that encourages us to live courageously, trusting Him in every circumstance.

Strategies for Overcoming Fear Through Faith

Overcoming fear is a process that requires intentionality, practice, and reliance on God. Below are strategies grounded in Scripture and practical wisdom to help you navigate fear with faith:

1. Acknowledge Your Fear

Recognize and Acknowledge:

- **Name your fears.** Express your anxieties. What specific things are you afraid of? Writing them down can help you externalize them and diminish their power. Take time to identify these fears without judgment.

- **Acknowledge their presence:** Don't try to suppress or ignore your fears. Instead, acknowledge them honestly and compassionately. Denial or suppression of fear often gives it more power. Instead, bring your fears to God in prayer.

As David wrote in Psalm 34:4, "I sought the Lord, and He answered me; He delivered me from all my fears." Naming your fears allows you to confront them with God's help and be reminded of His sovereignty over every situation.

Denying or suppressing fear often amplifies its hold over us, allowing it to grow unchecked. Instead, Scripture encourages us to bring our fears before God in prayer. By naming your fears, you take the first step in confronting them openly and seeking God's intervention. David's heartfelt proclamation in Psalm 34:4, "I sought the Lord, and He answered me; He delivered me from all my fears," reminds us of the power of turning to God with complete honesty. Through prayer, you invite Him to work in your heart, replace fear with His peace, and remind you of His sovereignty over all situations. Transparent prayer builds trust and reinforces the truth that God is always near, ready to provide His comfort and deliverance.

2. Meditate on God's Promises

- **Replace fear-based thoughts with truth-based affirmations.** One of the most powerful ways to combat fear is to actively replace negative, fear-based thoughts with the truth found in God's Word. Instead of dwelling on "what ifs" or uncertainties, shift your focus to God's promises and the strengths He has already instilled in you. This intentional mental shift can help displace anxiety and foster a mindset rooted in faith and hope.

- **Meditate on Scripture:** Set aside time each day to reflect on Bible verses that comfort and encourage you. Verses like Isaiah 41:10—"Do not fear, for I am with you; do not be dismayed, for I am your God"—serve as steady reminders of God's presence and unwavering support. By meditating on these truths, you train your mind and spirit to depend on Him rather than on fleeting emotions or external circumstances.

- **Surround yourself with truth: Be** mindful of the messages and content you allow into your life. Limit your exposure to negativity, whether through media, conversations, or personal thoughts, and instead seek out sources of inspiration and hope. Fill your environment with uplifting resources like worship music, sermons, or faith-centered books that point you back to God's promises. Creating a space focused on truth and positivity reinforces faith and helps you remain anchored in God's unchanging character, even when faced with challenges.

Fear frequently feeds on falsehoods and magnified scenarios, distorting your outlook and triggering unwarranted concern. Combat these fears by turning to the truth found in Scripture. God's Word is a powerful weapon to dismantle the lies fear tells. Verses like "I can do all things through Christ who strengthens me" (Philippians 4:13) remind us of the strength and support God provides. Similarly, meditating on passages such as, "The Lord is my light and my salvation—whom shall I fear?" (Psalm 27:1) affirms His sovereignty and loving care over every aspect of our lives. Embrace His promises and saturate your mind with His truth to replace fear with unwavering faith and confidence in His steadfast character.

3. Take Small Steps of Faith

- **Start small.** Take small, manageable steps to move closer to your goals. Whether it's reaching out to someone, committing to daily prayer, or volunteering in a new capacity, each small victory builds momentum and strengthens your confidence in God's plan for your life.

- **Embrace discomfort:** Growth often occurs outside our comfort zones. Challenge yourself to step outside your familiar boundaries and trust that God is guiding you through uncertainty. When you take steps of faith despite fear, you create opportunities for God to work powerfully in your life.
- **Celebrate your progress:** Acknowledge and celebrate your achievements, no matter how small. Every step forward, no matter how insignificant it might seem, is a testament to your faith and obedience. Commending progress bolsters your bravery, fosters endurance, and recalls God's faithfulness at every juncture of your journey.

Take time to acknowledge and celebrate your achievements, no matter how small they may appear. Every stride, no matter how small, serves as a profound testament to your faith and commitment. These milestones, however minor, signify progress and reflect your commitment to the journey God has set before you.

Celebrating your progress is more than just a moment of joy—it reinforces your courage, fuels your perseverance, and serves as a reminder of God's faithfulness. By recognizing His hand in every stage of your journey, you honor the growth He is cultivating within you.

Remember, even the smallest victories are part of the larger tapestry of God's purpose for your life. Take heart, celebrate often, and let these moments inspire you to press on with confidence and hope.

4. Seek Support and Encouragement from Others

- **Connect with others who share your faith:** Building relationships with fellow believers can provide immense support and encouragement along your faith journey. Share your struggles openly and celebrate victories together. A supportive community not only uplifts you in times of difficulty but also helps to strengthen your faith through shared experiences and collective prayer.

- **Seek guidance from mentors:** Finding a trusted mentor or spiritual advisor can be invaluable. A mentor can offer wisdom rooted in scripture, personal experience, and a deep understanding of God's word. They can encourage you during challenging times, provide accountability, and help you stay grounded in your spiritual walk. Establishing such relationships can nurture your growth and provide practical insight as you continue your journey of faith.

The company you keep has a profound impact on your spiritual walk. Seek relationships with individuals who inspire you, challenge you, and encourage your faith. Proverbs 27:17 reminds us, "As iron sharpens iron, so one person sharpens another." Establish connections with reliable friends or mentors who can accompany you, providing prayer, encouragement, and godly insights. Openly sharing your fears and challenges with them creates room for significant support and truth to influence your life positively. These relationships can serve as a steady source of strength and direction as you grow closer to God.

5. Remember Past Victories

Reflecting on the importance of faith and trust in God can greatly strengthen you for future challenges. When David faced Goliath, his confidence came from remembering how God had helped him defeat the lion and the bear (1 Samuel 17:37). To provide context, David was a young shepherd who tended his father's sheep. While protecting the flock, he encountered life-threatening situations, including attacks from a lion and a bear. With God's help, David overcame these predators, an experience that prepared him for future challenges.

Later, when the giant Goliath—a fierce Philistine warrior—threatened Israel's army, David volunteered to fight him. While others were paralyzed by fear, David's trust in God gave him boldness. He declared that just as God had delivered him from the lion and the bear, He would deliver him from Goliath. Armed with a slingshot and five stones, David struck down the giant, demonstrating that faith in God's past deliverance can empower us to face overwhelming obstacles.

David's story powerfully reminds us to reflect on how God has helped us overcome difficulties in the past. This can strengthen our faith and courage, assuring us that He remains faithful in every season of our lives. Reflecting on past victories gave David the courage to confront the giant with unwavering trust in God, knowing that the same God who helped him before would be with him in this new challenge.

For instance, recall a time when you prayed for guidance in a challenging situation, and God provided you with clarity and direction, guiding you through the difficulty. Recalling that specific moment can motivate you to trust Him in your present challenges. Keeping a journal of answered prayers and past victories can be a valuable tool in times of uncertainty, providing you with a tangible record of God's faithfulness and a source of strength during challenging times. This practice allows you to reflect on God's provision and power, strengthening your faith in His unwavering faithfulness as you see His hand at work in your life through answered prayers and victories.

By intentionally recalling God's faithfulness, you empower yourself to face new challenges with increased courage, knowing that the same God who was faithful in the past will continue to be by your side. This reminder reinforces that just as God has been with you in the past, He is with you now, guiding you through every trial, and will continue to be your steadfast companion in the journey of faith.

6. Surrender Control to God

- **Release control:** One of the most challenging yet freeing steps in overcoming life's uncertainties is surrendering control to God. Release your anxieties by laying them at His feet, trusting in His perfect timing and plan. This act of surrender acknowledges that His ways are higher than ours and that He sees the bigger picture we cannot fully grasp.

- **Practice patience:** Practice patience as you wait for His promises to unfold. Keep in mind that positive outcomes often require time, and God consistently operates in the background for your advantage (Romans 8:28). Trust in His ability to work all things together for your good, even when the process feels slow or unclear. Surrendering to God not only brings peace but also allows you to walk in faith, knowing that He is in control and His plans are always for your ultimate good.

Fear often arises when we try to control outcomes, clinging to our own plans and understanding instead of trusting in God's wisdom. True faith requires us to surrender these plans and place our confidence in His perfect timing and infinite knowledge. Proverbs 3:5-6 reminds us to "Trust in the Lord with all your heart and lean not on your own understanding; in all your ways submit to Him, and He will make your paths straight."

Overcoming fear is not a one-time achievement but an ongoing journey of growth. It demands consistent effort, steadfast faith, and a willingness to step forward into the unknown, trusting that God is already there. While this path may be difficult, take heart in knowing that you are never walking it alone. God is with you every step of the way, offering His unwavering presence, strength, and courage to help you face whatever challenges come your way.

Examples of Faith Conquering Fear

- **Moses and the Red Sea:** When the Israelites faced the Red Sea with Pharaoh's army closing in, fear overwhelmed them. They saw no way out and felt trapped by their circumstances. However, Moses placed his trust in God's power and proclaimed, "The Lord will fight for you; you need only to be still" (Exodus 14:14). God responded by parting the sea, allowing the Israelites to escape, and demonstrating that faith in Him can triumph over even the most daunting fears.
- **Jesus in Gethsemane:** Even Jesus, in His humanity, experienced deep anguish and fear in the Garden of Gethsemane as He prepared to face the cross. He confessed to His disciples, "My soul is overwhelmed with sorrow to the point of death" (Matthew 26:38). Yet, through heartfelt prayer, He submitted to God's will, saying, "Not as I will, but as you will" (Matthew 26:39). This moment reveals that courage is not the absence of fear but choosing obedience and trust in God even when the path ahead seems overwhelming.
- **Paul's Perseverance in Trials:** The Apostle Paul faced immense challenges and hardships, including imprisonment, beatings, and constant threats to his life. Yet, he remained steadfast in his faith and mission, declaring, "We are hard pressed on every side, but not crushed; perplexed, but not

> in despair; persecuted, but not abandoned; struck down, but not destroyed" (2 Corinthians 4:8–9). Paul's unwavering trust in God's strength and purpose serves as a powerful example of resilience, showing that even in the midst of overwhelming trials, faith enables believers to persevere and find hope.

These examples demonstrate how faith conquers fear and changes our view of challenges. It allows us to trust in God's power and His plans, even when they may seem impossible or uncertain. Surrendering to Him enables us to experience His strength, peace, and courage in the face of fear, giving us the ability to overcome obstacles and grow in our faith journey. May we continue to surrender to God daily, trusting in His perfect love that casts out all fear (1 John 4:18) and embracing His promises with unwavering faith. So let us continue walking this journey of faith together, hand in hand with the Creator who will never forsake us.

Encouragement to Embrace Courageous Faith

Fear is a natural part of life, but it does not have to define you. Through faith in God, you can confront your fears, overcome obstacles, and walk in the boldness He desires for you. God's strength is made perfect in our weakness, and His presence empowers us to step forward with courage. Remember, just as Jesus calmed the storm for the disciples on the Sea of Galilee (Mark 4:35–41), He is present in the midst of your storms, offering His peace that surpasses understanding and the victory over every fear. He has pledged to never abandon us, and His unwavering love dispels all fear.

Let the words of 2 Chronicles 20:15 strengthen your heart: "Do not be afraid or discouraged because of this vast army. For the battle is not yours, but God's." Just as He fought for His people in times past, He stands ready to fight for you today. The journey to courageous faith is challenging but worthwhile. God has equipped you with His Spirit, His Word, and His promises to face whatever comes your way. You are never alone, for He walks with you every step of the way. Believe in His plan, find peace in His presence, and remember that He is the ultimate victor. Let faith lead you, not fear.

CHAPTER 3
FAITH IN ACTION

Overview: This chapter explores the transformative impact of putting faith into action and how it honors God.

Courageous faith requires action—bold, intentional steps that explicitly reflect our trust in God and His promises. It's one thing to say we believe; it's another to let that belief shape our decisions and propel us forward, especially when the path ahead is unclear. This chapter explores the profound impact of putting faith into action and the ways it brings honor to God.

At its core, faith is not simply a passive belief but an active trust and belief in God's promises. It's a dynamic force that demands action. True faith goes beyond intellectual agreement; it is a dynamic, living expression that results in tangible acts of obedience. James 2:26 emphasizes the inseparable link between faith and action, highlighting that genuine faith is evidenced through works, such as acts of kindness, obedience, and service. This verse calls us to a steadfast commitment where our words are matched by our deeds. It challenges us to step out of our comfort zones, trusting that God will meet us where we are and guide us as we go.

Acting in faith aligns us with God's will, enabling His power to operate within and through us, guiding our steps and empowering us to fulfill His purposes. From small acts of kindness to extraordinary leaps of trust, every step of faith is a declaration of our reliance on Him. Biblical examples, such as Peter stepping out of the boat to walk on water or Abraham leaving his homeland without knowing his destination, remind us of the miraculous outcomes that follow faithful action. Though the path may not always be clear, the God who calls us is faithful.

Through faith in action, we begin to see life from a heavenly perspective. Challenges, such as facing adversity or uncertainty, become opportunities for God's glory to be seen, showcasing His faithfulness and provision in unexpected ways. Acting on our faith not only deepens our connection with the Creator but also fortifies the core principles that underpin our lives.

The Relationship Between Faith and Action

This section explores the interconnected relationship between faith and action in fulfilling God's purposes.

James 2:17 emphasizes that faith without corresponding actions is inactive and lacks vitality, illustrating the importance of action in giving life to faith and yielding significant results. Genuine faith is not passive or stagnant; it is alive, dynamic, and transformative, shaping our attitudes, decisions, and interactions with others. **Faith compels us to respond by trusting God enough to take steps forward,**

even when the path ahead is unclear, like Abraham leaving his homeland or Peter stepping out of the boat onto the water.

When God calls us to act, He doesn't promise that the journey will be easy, but He does assure us of His presence and provision, sustaining us through difficulties and guiding us with His wisdom. Acting in faith means stepping out in obedience, even when circumstances seem overwhelming or the outcome is uncertain. **Faith is more than just acknowledging God's ability; it involves living with full confidence that He will fulfill what He has promised.**

Courageous faith bridges the gap between trusting God and taking action to fulfill His plans. It is the faith that moved **Abraham** to leave his homeland without knowing where he was going, trusting that God would lead him (Hebrews 11:8). It is the faith that enabled **Peter** to step out of the boat and walk on water toward Jesus, even when the storm raged around him (Matthew 14:29).

Acting in faith involves aligning our decisions and actions with God's will, with the assurance that He will lead and direct our paths. When we act on our faith, we invite God to move in powerful ways, making the impossible possible. **Engaging in faith-filled actions distinguishes between passive belief and actively living out the calling God has placed on our lives.**

So, what is God asking you to step into today? What specific act of obedience is He inviting you to embrace? Perhaps He is calling you to start a new ministry, reach out to someone in need, forgive a past hurt, or take a bold step in your career. Maybe He is asking you to trust Him with a difficult situation, even when the outcome is uncertain.

For example, imagine God placing it on your heart to mentor a young believer, but you feel unqualified. Instead of allowing fear to hold you back, take the first step—reach out, offer encouragement, and trust that God will equip you along the way. Or perhaps He is leading you to leave behind a comfort zone and embark on a new journey, much like Abraham, who stepped out in faith without knowing where God would take him (Hebrews 11:8).

As you trust in Him and move forward, remember that faith partnered with action unlocks the fullness of God's promises. Every step of obedience, no matter how small, brings you closer to His divine purpose for your life. Step forward boldly, knowing that He is with you every step of the way, strengthening and guiding you.

Biblical Examples of Obedience Despite Uncertainty

The Bible is filled with stories of men and women who demonstrated unwavering obedience despite the uncertainty before them. **These individuals didn't always have clear answers, immediate rewards, or guaranteed outcomes, but they chose to trust God and follow His direction.** Their faith-driven actions serve as timeless reminders that God honors those who trust and obey Him, even when the path ahead is unknown.

1. Noah Building the Ark: A Testament to Courageous Faith

Noah's story is one of the most powerful examples of courageous faith in action. **When God commanded him to build an ark in preparation for a great flood, it was an unprecedented instruction—one that defied human logic and understanding.** Yet, Noah did not question or hesitate; he obeyed wholeheartedly.

Genesis 6:22 records Noah's unwavering faith:

"Noah did everything just as God commanded him."

At the time, there was no sign of a flood, and the idea of a massive vessel built on dry land seemed absurd to those around him. Noah endured ridicule, skepticism, and likely social isolation, yet he remained steadfast in his obedience. **His faith was not shaken by the disbelief**

of others because his trust was anchored in God's Word, not human approval.

Faith in Action Requires Perseverance

Noah's obedience was not a one-time decision but a lifelong commitment. **It took years, perhaps decades, to complete the ark.** Day after day, he labored, trusting that God's promise would come to pass, even when there was no visible evidence.

His perseverance teaches us:

- **Faith requires endurance.** Sometimes, God's promises take time to unfold, and obedience may demand patience.

- **Faith demands standing strong in the face of challenges.** Like Noah, we may face doubt or criticism when we follow God's calling, but obedience must outweigh fear of rejection.

- **Faith requires trusting in the unseen.** Hebrews 11:7 affirms Noah's faith, stating:
  "By faith Noah, when warned about things not yet seen, in holy fear built an ark to save his family."

Noah's Legacy of Obedience

Noah's faith did not just impact his own life—it preserved his family, humanity, and countless species of animals. His obedience led to God's covenant, a promise symbolized by the rainbow (Genesis 9:12-17), reassuring us that God is faithful to His word.

Noah's story reminds us that acting in faith often requires perseverance, especially when others fail to understand or support our obedience to God's call. Even when we don't see immediate results, **our faith in action can have lasting effects, shaping generations and fulfilling God's greater plan.**

Like Noah, may we choose faith over doubt, obedience over fear, and perseverance over discouragement. **Even when the world does not understand, God sees, honors, and blesses those who trust in Him.** What step of faith is God calling you to take today? Will you, like Noah, choose obedience despite uncertainty?

2. Abraham Offering Isaac: A Profound Act of Faith.

One of the most heart-wrenching and powerful acts of faith recorded in Scripture is **Abraham's willingness to sacrifice his son, Isaac, in obedience to God's command.** This test of faith was beyond human comprehension—Isaac was not just Abraham's beloved son; he was the child of promise, the one through whom God had vowed to establish a great nation (Genesis 12:2-3).

Yet, despite the incomprehensible nature of God's request, **Abraham trusted in God's faithfulness and obeyed without hesitation.** Genesis 22:3 tells us that early the next morning, Abraham set out for Mount Moriah, taking Isaac with him for the sacrifice. There is no record of him questioning God or seeking an alternative—only unwavering faith in the One who had always kept His promises.

Faith in the Face of the Impossible

Abraham's faith was not blind; it was deeply rooted in **his belief that God's promises would never fail.** Hebrews 11:19 gives us insight into Abraham's thoughts:

"Abraham reasoned that God could even raise the dead, and in a sense, he did receive Isaac back from death."

Even in the face of what seemed like an unbearable command, Abraham believed that God could restore Isaac's life if necessary. His trust in God was so complete that **he walked up the mountain with faith, declaring to his servants, "We will worship and then we will come back to you" (Genesis 22:5).** This was a declaration of confidence that Isaac would return with him, one way or another.

God's Miraculous Provision

At the moment when Abraham was about to sacrifice Isaac, **God intervened.** A voice from heaven called out, stopping him, and a ram was provided as a substitute offering (Genesis 22:12-13). This moment not only demonstrated God's provision but also foreshadowed the ultimate sacrifice—**Jesus Christ, the Lamb of God, who would be given as a substitute for the sins of humanity.**

Genesis 22:14 records Abraham naming the place "Jehovah Jireh," meaning "The Lord Will Provide." This name serves as a timeless reminder that **God always provides what is needed when we trust and obey Him.**

The Legacy of Abraham's Faith

Because of Abraham's obedience, **God reaffirmed His covenant, promising that his descendants would be as numerous as the stars in the sky and that through him, all nations would be blessed (Genesis 22:16-18).** Abraham's faith was not only tested but also rewarded, as his obedience paved the way for God's redemptive plan to unfold.

Lessons from Abraham's Faith

1. **Faith requires trust beyond human understanding.** Abraham believed in God's faithfulness even when the command seemed impossible.
2. **Obedience precedes provision.** Abraham obeyed first, and God provided the ram as a sacrifice.
3. **God is faithful to His promises.** Even when the path is uncertain, He never fails to fulfill His word.
4. **God's tests are opportunities for deeper faith.** Abraham's trial refined his trust in God, revealing His character in an even greater way.

A Call to Trust and Obedience

Abraham's story challenges you to examine your own faith. **Are we willing to trust God completely, even when His plans seem unclear?** Do we have confidence that **He will provide, even when we don't see a way forward?**

While God may not put us through the same trials as Abraham, He does call us to relinquish our own "Isaacs"—the things we cherish most—and to fully trust Him. Just as Abraham's willingness to let go led to an even greater blessing, our obedience to God's leading paves the way for His miraculous work in our lives.

Like Abraham, **let us walk in faith, trusting that Jehovah Jireh, our Provider, will always make a way.**

3. The Widow of Zarephath: A Small Act of Faith with a Miraculous Reward

The story of **the widow of Zarephath** is a powerful example of how faith, even in the smallest of actions, can lead to divine provision. This account, found in 1 Kings 17:7-16, demonstrates how obedience, even in the face of desperation, can unlock God's miraculous blessings.

A Test of Faith in the Midst of Desperation

During a severe drought and famine, the prophet **Elijah** was sent by God to Zarephath, where he encountered a widow gathering sticks. She was preparing to make a final meal for herself and her son before they would succumb to starvation. Her situation was dire—she had nothing left but **a handful of flour and a little oil.**

Yet, despite her hopeless circumstances, **Elijah made a bold request.** He asked her to first make him a small loaf of bread before preparing food for herself and her son. This must have seemed unreasonable; after all, she barely had enough for her family. But **Elijah assured her with God's promise**:

"For this is what the Lord, the God of Israel, says: 'The jar of flour will not be used up and the jug of oil will not run dry until the day the Lord sends rain on the land.'" – **1 Kings 17:14**

Obedience that Unlocked Provision

In an incredible act of faith, the widow chose to obey. She prepared the bread for Elijah first, trusting in the prophet's words. **Her obedience led to a supernatural provision—her flour and oil never ran out for the entire duration of the famine!**

"She went away and did as Elijah had told her. So there was food every day for Elijah and for the woman and her family." – **1 Kings 17:15**

This miracle shows that **even the smallest acts of faith can bring about extraordinary blessings.** The widow gave out of her lack, and in return, God provided for her abundantly.

Lessons from the Widow's Faith

1. **Faith often requires sacrifice.** The widow had to let go of what little she had to experience God's provision.

2. **God sees our needs and provides.** Even in a drought, God sustained her because of her trust in Him.

3. **Obedience activates God's miracles.** The moment she acted on God's word, her situation changed.

4. God demonstrates His power in unexpected ways. A poor widow became an example of unwavering faith and divine blessing.

A Call to Trust God's Provision

Like the widow of Zarephath, we may sometimes feel like we have little to give—whether it's resources, strength, or hope. But God is asking us to trust Him, even with our **last bit of "flour and oil."** When we act in faith, **He is faithful to provide, sustain, and bless beyond what we can imagine.**

Are you holding back something because you fear lack? **Trust that when you put God first, He will always take care of you.** As Jesus later affirmed in **Luke 4:25-26**, this widow's faith was recognized and honored by God.

Let us follow her example and take bold steps of faith, knowing that **God's provision is always enough, and His promises never fail.**

1. **Abraham's Journey of Faith: A Life Marked by Obedience and Trust**

2. **A Call to the Unknown (Genesis 12:1-4)Faith Tested Through Trials (Genesis 12-21)The Ultimate Test of Faith: Offering Isaac (Genesis 22)Lessons from Abraham's Faith JourneyA Call to Walk in Abraham's FootstepsAbraham's life (Genesis 12-22) is one of the greatest examples of faith in action.** His obedience to God's call, even in the face of uncertainty, trials, and tests, reveals the power of unwavering trust in divine promises. His journey demonstrates that faith is not about possessing all the answers, but about placing your trust in the One who possesses them.

Abraham's faith journey began when
God commanded him to leave his homeland, his family, and everything familiar to travel to a foreign land.

Bringing Your Beliefs to Life Through Faith

These biblical narratives underscore a crucial truth: **faith without action is dead** (James 2:17). Faith is like a **dormant seed**—full of potential but incapable of producing fruit unless it is nurtured and activated. **True faith is not just believing in God's promises; it**

is stepping forward in obedience, trusting that He will fulfill them. For instance, when faced with a difficult decision, true faith involves following God's guidance even when it seems challenging.

So, how do we translate this principle into our own lives? **How do we take bold, faith-filled actions that honor God and bring glory to His name?** Here are a few practical steps:

1. **Discern God's Will:**
    - **Spend time in prayer:** Begin by seeking God's guidance through prayer and meditation. Quiet your heart and mind, allowing space to hear His voice and sense His direction. Prayer is a vital connection that invites God into every decision, providing clarity and peace.
    - **Study His Word:** Immerse yourself in Scripture, letting God's truth illuminate your path. The Bible serves as a lamp to your feet and a light to your path (Psalm 119:105), offering wisdom and insight that align your choices with His will.
    - **Seek wise counsel:** Surround yourself with trusted mentors and spiritual advisors who can provide guidance and discernment. Proverbs 15:22 reminds us, *"Plans fail for lack of counsel, but with many advisers, they succeed."* The perspectives of godly individuals can help confirm what God is revealing to you.
2. **Step Out in Faith:**
    - Embrace the unknown: Following God's guidance often necessitates venturing beyond your comfort zone

and welcoming uncertainty. Trusting Him means being willing to walk paths you may not fully understand, knowing that His plans are greater than your own (Isaiah 55:8-9).

- **Take the first step:** The most challenging part of any journey is often the beginning. Take that initial step in faith, even if it feels small or insignificant. As you move forward, trust that God will provide the strength and resources you need for the journey ahead.

- **Focus on obedience, not outcomes:** Instead of fixating on the desired results, concentrate on being obedient to God's will. True faith is about surrendering the outcome to Him, confident that His plans are for your good and His glory (Romans 8:28).

3. **Persevere in the Face of Challenges:**

   - **Obstacles are expected; challenges are part of the faith journey.** Understanding this helps you prepare your heart and mind to face difficulties with resilience and trust in God's plan. Remember, trials are often opportunities for growth and refinement.

   - **Draw strength from God's promises:** When difficulties arise, anchor yourself in God's promises. Reflect on His faithfulness and His unwavering commitment to His children. Scriptures like Isaiah 41:10 remind us, *"Do not fear, for I am with you; do not be dismayed, for I am your God. I will strengthen you and help you."* Make His Word your source of strength and hope, guiding you in times of need.

- **Learn from your mistakes:** Every setback carries an opportunity for growth. Instead of dwelling on failures, seek the lessons they offer. Allow God to use your mistakes to teach you, refine you, and strengthen your faith for the journey ahead.

4. **Trust in God's Provision:**

    - **Release your anxieties:** Surrender your worries and burdens to God, trusting in His provision and guidance. Philippians 4:6-7 reminds us, *"Do not be anxious about anything, but in every situation, by prayer and petition, with thanksgiving, present your requests to God. And the peace of God, which transcends all understanding, will guard your hearts and your minds in Christ Jesus."* Let go of fear and embrace His peace.

    - **Live by faith, not by sight:** True faith is trusting in God's promises, even when circumstances seem uncertain or discouraging. As stated in 2 Corinthians 5:7, we trust in what we cannot see, not what is visible. Even when you can't see the path ahead, have faith that God is working in the background for your benefit.

    - **Be grateful for every blessing:** Cultivate a heart of gratitude, recognizing and appreciating the many blessings God provides daily. Gratitude shifts your focus from what is lacking to what God has already done, reinforcing your trust in His continued faithfulness.

However, taking bold actions of faith may not always be easy. It requires courage, perseverance, and a deep reliance on God's grace. Trusting Him means stepping beyond fear and uncertainty, believing that He will guide and sustain us through every challenge.

Yet, the rewards of faith-filled obedience are immeasurable. As we step out in faith, we experience profound personal transformation—our trust in God deepens, our character strengthens, and our purpose becomes clearer. More importantly, our faith-driven actions allow us to become instruments of God's love and grace in the world. Through our obedience, He works in and through us to impact others, bringing hope, healing, and encouragement where it is needed most.

So take heart, be courageous, and step forward in faith. God is with you every step of the way, and His plans for you are greater than you can imagine.

Practical Steps to Take Bold, Faith-Filled Actions

While the examples of Noah building the ark, Abraham leaving his homeland, or Esther approaching the king may seem extraordinary, the principles of faith in action are deeply relevant to our everyday lives. Here are practical steps to help you take bold, faith-filled actions:

1. Listen for God's Voice: Begin each day with prayer and meditation, seeking guidance on important decisions. For example, before accepting a job offer, take time to pray and listen for God's direction. Faith-filled action begins with discerning God's will. This requires intentionally seeking His guidance through prayer and the study of Scripture. Spending time in God's presence helps align your heart with His purposes and provides clarity for the path ahead.

As Psalm 119:105 reminds us, *"Your word is a lamp to my feet, a light on my path."* God's Word illuminates the steps He wants you to take, offering wisdom and assurance even in uncertain circumstances. Trust that as you seek Him, God will reveal His will in His perfect timing. While waiting for His direction, it's important to stay attentive to the ways He may be guiding you. God's guidance can be revealed through various channels such as prayer, Scripture, wise counsel, inner peace, or unexpected openings and closings.

An effective way to discern God's timing is to seek confirmation through His Word. If a decision aligns with biblical principles and brings peace rather than confusion, it may be a sign that God is guiding you forward. Additionally, circumstances may shift in ways that affirm or redirect your path. Sometimes, delays are not denials but divine preparation for what's ahead.

For example, if you are praying about a major life decision—such as a career change or ministry opportunity—pay attention to recurring messages in Scripture, godly advice from trusted mentors, and a deep sense of peace when considering a particular direction. If uncertainty lingers, it may be a call to wait and trust in His timing.

Listen attentively and move forward in confidence, knowing that God is faithfully guiding you. His plans are always for your good, and He will make the right path clear in due time.

2. Take the First Step, Even If It's Small Often, the most challenging aspect of acting in faith is taking the initial step. Like Peter stepping out of the boat to walk on water toward Jesus (Matthew 14:29), that initial move may feel risky and uncertain. However, it is also a profound act of trust in God's faithfulness.

Don't wait for every detail to be perfectly clear before moving forward. Faith often requires stepping into the unknown, believing that God will provide guidance and strength along the way. As you walk in obedience, He will direct your path and equip you for the journey ahead, providing strength, wisdom, and discernment along the way. Each step, no matter how small, is significant when taken in faith.

3. Surround Yourself with Support Faith-filled action is not meant to be a solo journey. God often uses the support of others to strengthen and encourage us along the way. Engage with a community of believers who can provide encouragement, prayer support, and accountability to help you align with God's purpose.

Proverbs 27:17 reminds us, *"As iron sharpens iron, so one person sharpens another."* Engaging with a faith-filled community provides perspective, wisdom, and motivation, helping you stay focused and resilient. Together, you can build each other up, celebrating victories and persevering through challenges as you follow God's lead.

4. Reflect on God's Faithfulness When fear or doubt begins to creep in, take time to reflect on God's past faithfulness. Remembering how He has provided, guided, and delivered you in previous situations can strengthen your resolve to act in faith.

A practical approach is to maintain a journal documenting answered prayers and past victories for personal reflection. Reviewing these reminders of God's provision can help you see His hand at work, even in challenging circumstances. As you reflect on His unchanging faithfulness, your trust in Him will grow, giving you the courage to step forward in faith with confidence.

5. Prepare for Resistance Taking bold steps of faith often brings resistance. This opposition may come from external circumstances, the doubts or criticisms of others, or even your own insecurities. It's important to recognize that challenges are a natural part of stepping out in faith.

Ephesians 6:10-11 reminds us to, *"Be strong in the Lord and in His mighty power. Put on the full armor of God, so that you can take your stand against the devil's schemes."* By equipping yourself with the truth of God's Word, prayer, and the support of fellow believers, you can stand firm in the face of adversity.

Expect challenges, but don't be discouraged. Trust that God will strengthen and equip you to overcome them, allowing your faith to grow even stronger through the process.

6. Trust in God's Timing Faith-filled action does not always yield immediate results. There may be seasons of waiting, during which trusting in God's perfect timing becomes essential. His plans are designed for your ultimate good and are far greater than what you can imagine (Jeremiah 29:11).

Be patient and persistent as you walk in obedience, even when you don't see immediate outcomes. Trust that every step you take in faith is part of a bigger plan that will bear fruit in His appointed time. Waiting is not a hindrance to God's purpose; it is a period of preparation and growth for the future.

Encouragement to Live Faith in Action

Take a bold step of faith today, whether it's reaching out to someone in need or starting a new venture. Trust in God's guidance and believe that He will work through you to impact the world around you.

Faith in action transforms ordinary lives into extraordinary testimonies of God's power. It is not about living without fear, but about choosing to be faithful despite it. As you step out in obedience, remember the promise of God: *"My grace is sufficient for you, for my power is made perfect in weakness"* (2 Corinthians 12:9). When you feel unsure, rely on God's strength to support you.

Reflect on Jesus' words that whoever believes in Him will do greater works than He did, as He is going to the Father (John 14:12). Through faith-filled action, you can partner with God in fulfilling His purposes on earth, presenting a remarkable opportunity. Even the smallest acts of faith can result in extraordinary outcomes that bring glory to God.

Take courage and press forward with the assurance of Philippians 4:13: "I can do all things through Christ who strengthens me." Trust that God is with you every step of the way. Trust that God is with you, empowering and guiding you every step of the way, whether your step of faith is as simple as offering encouragement to someone in need or as monumental as starting a new ministry.

Now is the time to take action. What bold move will you make today?

CHAPTER 4

NAVIGATING PAIN AND FORGIVENESS

Pain is an inevitable part of life. It can leave lasting wounds in our hearts, whether the cause is betrayal, loss, or unmet expectations. Yet, within the storm of pain lies an opportunity for healing and freedom through forgiveness. Forgiveness means deciding to release the bitterness and resentment in our hearts, instead of ignoring the harm caused to us. This chapter explores the power of forgiveness, how it contributes to personal growth, and the biblical guidance that assists us in navigating this transformative journey.

These experiences, while painful, offer profound opportunities for growth and transformation. At the heart of this transformative process lies the powerful act of forgiveness. Forgiveness involves releasing the grip of bitterness and resentment that binds us, not condoning the actions of others.

Forgiveness connects us with God's love and His call to show grace to others. The Bible stresses the significance of forgiving others as we have been forgiven by God. **Ephesians 4:32** reminds us, *"Be kind* *to one another, tenderhearted, forgiving one another, as God in Christ forgave you."*

A powerful biblical example of forgiveness is found in the story of **Jesus on the cross**. Even when falsely accused, beaten, and crucified, Jesus showed grace to those who harmed Him, saying, "Father, forgive them, for they do not know what they are doing" (Luke 23:34). His ultimate act of love demonstrates that forgiveness is not about who deserves it but about reflecting God's mercy.

Forgiving mirrors God's love, inviting His healing power into our hearts. Forgiveness releases us from resentment, improves our relationships, and brings us nearer to God's heart. It is through this act of kindness that we truly reflect the character of Christ in our lives.

The process of forgiveness requires vulnerability, honest reflection, and ongoing reliance on prayer and faith. However, as we take each step toward forgiveness, we invite peace into our lives and make room for reconciliation and renewal. Forgiveness is a gift to others and a liberating act for oneself. Forgiveness helps us let go of the burden of pain, leading to a lighter heart and the ability to embrace the joy and hope promised by God.

The Power of Forgiveness: Freeing Your Heart from Bitterness

Forgiveness is commonly misinterpreted. It does not involve erasing the pain or pretending the hurt didn't occur. Instead, forgiveness is an act of grace—choosing to let go of the anger and resentment that weigh us down.

Holding onto anger and resentment is like ingesting poison and expecting the other person to suffer. It corrodes our inner peace, fuels negativity, and hinders our ability to experience joy and fulfillment.

Forgiveness, on the other hand, is an act of self-liberation. It breaks the chains of bitterness, allowing us to reclaim our emotional and spiritual freedom.

Carrying a heavy burden of unforgiveness poisons our spirit. Bitterness has the power to consume us, robbing us of joy, peace, and even physical health. Hebrews 12:15 warns us, “See to it that no one falls short of the grace of God and that no bitter root grows up to cause trouble and defile many.”

Forgiveness liberates us from the chains of bitterness, enabling us to encounter the peace that comes from God. It is a gift we give ourselves as much as it is a response to others. Jesus’ teaching in Matthew 6:14-15 reminds us of the importance of forgiveness: “For if you forgive other people when they sin against you, your heavenly Father will also forgive you. But if you do not forgive others their sins, your Father will not forgive your sins.”

When we forgive, we align ourselves with God's will and pave the way for healing and reconciliation. Forgiveness opens the door to restoration and renewal—not just in our relationships with others, but also in our relationship with God. Not just in our relationships with others, but also in our relationship with God, forgiveness paves the way for restoration and renewal.t God desires for each of us.

Personal Growth Through Letting Go of Past Hurts

Embarking on a journey of forgiveness leads to deep personal growth and transformation. When we choose to let go of past hurts, we create space for God to heal our hearts and work in our lives in new and meaningful ways.

- **Embracing Freedom:** Forgiveness liberates us from the heavy burden of anger, resentment, and pain. Holding onto past hurts keeps us trapped in the past, preventing us from fully embracing the future God has planned for us. Isaiah 43:18-19 reminds us, *"Forget the former things; do not dwell on the past. See, I am doing a new thing!"* When we release the past, we open ourselves to the fresh and beautiful work God wants to do in our lives.

- **Developing Empathy:** True forgiveness often requires us to extend grace to others, just as God has extended grace to us. When we remember how much we have been forgiven, we can more easily show mercy to those who have wronged us. Ephesians 4:32 encourages us, *"Be kind and compassionate to one another, forgiving each other, just as in Christ God forgave you."* Viewing others through the lens of grace fosters empathy, understanding, and a heart that mirrors Christ's love.

- **Strengthening Faith:** Choosing to forgive is an act of obedience and trust in God. It is a way of saying, *"Lord, I release this pain to You, trusting that You will bring justice and healing."* This surrender deepens our faith and allows us to experience God's peace and restoration. As we let go and trust in His perfect plan, we grow spiritually and strengthen our relationship with Him.

Forgiveness is often challenging, yet it is consistently enriching and transformative. As we release past hurts, we step into the freedom, healing, and transformation that God desires for us. Consider a concrete step you can take today to release the past and embrace the new opportunities God has prepared for you.

Biblical Guidance on Forgiveness: Joseph's Story

Few biblical stories illustrate forgiveness as powerfully as the story of Joseph. Betrayed by his own brothers, Joseph endured years of suffering—sold into slavery, falsely accused, and imprisoned.Yet, despite his pain, he chose forgiveness over revenge, demonstrating an unwavering trust in God's greater plan.

In Genesis 50:20, Joseph speaks profound words to his brothers: *"You intended to harm me, but God intended it for good to accomplish what is now being done, the saving of many lives."* His perspective reveals a deep faith in God's sovereignty and redemptive purposes.

Joseph's forgiveness not only freed him from bitterness but also restored his family and played a crucial role in preserving an entire nation. His story teaches us several key lessons about forgiveness:

- **Forgiveness is not denial:** Joseph did not ignore or excuse his brothers' actions. He acknowledged their wrongdoing but chose to respond with grace rather than resentment. True forgiveness does not minimize pain but releases the hold it has over our hearts.

- **God can redeem pain:** What others intend for harm, God can use for good. Joseph's suffering ultimately led to his rise in Egypt, positioning him to save countless lives during a famine. Our trials, too, can be transformed into testimonies of God's faithfulness when we choose to trust Him.

- **Forgiveness restores relationships:** By forgiving his brothers, Joseph not only found personal healing but also brought reconciliation to his family. Forgiveness has the power to mend broken relationships and create a legacy of peace for future generations.

Joseph's story exemplifies the power of forgiveness and faith. It challenges us to trust in God's greater plan, even when we have been deeply wronged. Reflect on who in your life you need to extend forgiveness to today.

Forgiveness is primarily about our own healing and freedom, rather than solely about the other person. When we choose to forgive, we take a powerful step toward emotional, spiritual, and relational well-being. Here's how forgiveness transforms our lives:

- **We release ourselves from the emotional burden of past hurts.** Holding onto anger, resentment, and bitterness only weighs us down, keeping us trapped in the pain of the past. These emotions can become a heavy burden that affects our well-being, relationships, and spiritual growth.

Forgiveness is essential for breaking free from these restrictions and experiencing emotional and spiritual freedom. By choosing to let go, we release ourselves from the emotional weight that hinders our peace and joy. We make room for healing, renewal, and the peace that only God can offer by releasing ourselves from the chains of the past.

- **Experience greater inner peace and tranquility:** Unforgiveness can create inner turmoil, weighing heavily on our hearts and minds. The pain of holding onto past hurts can rob us of joy, disrupt our peace, and keep us emotionally bound to the offense.

However, when we choose to forgive, we release that burden and invite God's peace into our lives. Forgiveness is not just about the other person—it is about freeing ourselves from the chains of resentment and stepping into the calm and freedom that only God can provide.

- **Improve our relationships:** Forgiveness has the power to mend broken relationships, restore trust, and strengthen our connections with others. When we choose to let go of resentment and extend grace, we create an environment where healing and reconciliation can take place.

Even if full reconciliation is not possible, a forgiving heart fosters healthier interactions and a spirit of grace. Instead of allowing past hurts to define our relationships, forgiveness enables us to approach others with love, patience, and understanding.

- **Cultivate empathy and compassion:** When we extend forgiveness, we open our hearts to a greater capacity for empathy and compassion. Forgiveness allows us to see beyond the offense and recognize the humanity in others—their struggles, weaknesses, and imperfections. Just as we have needed grace in our own lives, we begin to understand that others are in need of that same mercy.

By acknowledging our own shortcomings and receiving God's forgiveness, we are better equipped to extend kindness and understanding to those who have wronged us.

Colossians 3:12-13

reminds us,

"Therefore, as God's chosen people, holy and dearly loved, clothe yourselves with compassion, kindness, humility, gentleness, and patience. Bear with each other and forgive one another if any of you has a grievance against someone. Forgive as the Lord forgave you."

- **Unlock our potential for growth and healing:** Forgiveness is a gateway to personal transformation. When we release the past, we free ourselves to embrace a future filled with new possibilities. Letting go of resentment clears the path for emotional and spiritual growth, allowing us to fully step into the life that God has prepared for us.

Unforgiveness keeps us tethered to pain, limiting our ability to move forward. But when we choose to forgive, we break those chains and step into healing and renewal.

Isaiah 43:18-19

reminds us,

"Forget the former things; do not dwell on the past. See, I am doing a new thing! Now it springs up; do you not perceive it? I am making a way in the wilderness and streams in the wasteland."

Biblical Guidance on Forgiveness

The Bible offers profound insights into the importance of forgiveness, teaching us that it is not only an act of grace toward others but also a reflection of God's mercy toward us.

- **Forgiving Others Leads to Receiving God's Forgiveness: Matthew 6:14-15** teaches us a profound truth: *"For if you forgive men their trespasses, your heavenly Father will also forgive you. But if you do not forgive men their trespasses, neither will your heavenly Father forgive your trespasses."*

This passage underscores the deep connection between our willingness to forgive others and God's forgiveness toward us. Forgiveness is not just an act of kindness—it is a reflection of the grace we have received from God. When we hold onto resentment, we block the flow of His mercy in our lives.

- **The Parable of the Unforgiving Servant (Matthew 18:21-35):** In this parable, Jesus teaches a powerful lesson about forgiveness. A servant owed his master an enormous debt—so large that he could never repay it. Out of compassion, the master forgave the entire debt, releasing the servant from his obligation.

However, that same servant later encountered a fellow servant who owed him a much smaller amount. Instead of extending the same mercy he had received, he demanded full payment and had the man thrown into prison. When the master heard of this, he was angered and revoked the servant's forgiveness, holding him accountable for his unwillingness to show grace.

- **Joseph's Story: The Power of Forgiveness (Genesis 37-50):** Joseph's life is one of the most compelling biblical examples of forgiveness. Despite being betrayed by his own brothers, sold into slavery, and wrongfully imprisoned, Joseph chose to forgive rather than seek retribution.His faith in God's sovereignty allowed him to see beyond his suffering and recognize a greater purpose in his trials.

In

Genesis 50:20

Joseph tells his brothers:

"You intended to harm me, but God intended it for good to accomplish what is now being done, the saving of many lives."

The Journey of Forgiveness: Steps to Emotional and Spiritual Freedom

While forgiveness is a complex journey, breaking it down into practical steps can empower us to grasp and embrace it more fully. It requires:

1. **Humility to Acknowledge Our Vulnerabilities**
   True forgiveness begins with recognizing our own need for grace. It takes humility to admit that we have been hurt, that

we are not immune to pain, and that we too have needed forgiveness from God and others. **James 4:10** reminds us, *"Humble yourselves before the Lord, and he will lift you up."*

2. **Compassion to Offer Mercy**
Extending mercy to those who have wronged us is not about excusing their actions but about choosing grace over bitterness. When we forgive, we reflect **God's unconditional love**. **Luke 6:36** encourages us, *"Be merciful, just as your Father is merciful."*

3. **Courage to Let Go and Embrace Healing**
Releasing resentment is one of the hardest yet most liberating aspects of forgiveness. Holding onto anger can feel justified, but it ultimately weighs us down. **Isaiah 43:18-19** calls us to release the past: *"Forget the former things; do not dwell on the past. See, I am doing a new thing!"* Letting go makes space for God's healing power to renew our hearts.

While forgiveness is not always easy, it is a **necessary step toward emotional and spiritual freedom**. Choosing to forgive allows us to walk in peace, unburdened by past wounds, and open to the abundant life God has prepared for us. What step will you take today to move forward in your forgiveness journey?

The rewards of forgiveness are immeasurable. By choosing to forgive, we **break free from the chains of bitterness** that keep us trapped in pain. Forgiveness allows God to restore our hearts and renew our spirits, paving the way for healing. It instills a profound sense of peace, surpassing human comprehension, and infuses our lives with joy that remains independent of our circumstances.

Ultimately, forgiveness is not just a gift we give to others; it is a gift we give to ourselves. It empowers us to **move forward unburdened, embracing the abundant life** that God desires for us.

Today, take a step toward freedom. **Choose forgiveness, and experience the peace, joy, and healing that it brings.**

Practical Steps to Embrace Forgiveness

Forgiveness is frequently more challenging in practice than in theory. It is a journey that requires intentional effort, patience, and faith. Here are practical steps to help you navigate the process of forgiveness and experience healing:

1. Acknowledge the Pain Facing the pain head-on is the first step in forgiveness. Ignoring or suppressing hurt can make it fester, leading to bitterness and resentment. Instead, bring your pain before God in prayer, allowing Him to comfort and heal your heart.

Psalm 34:18 assures us, *"The Lord is close to the brokenhearted and saves those who are crushed in spirit."* God sees your pain, and He is ready to walk with you through the process of healing. When you acknowledge your hurt, you take the first step toward releasing it.

True forgiveness does not mean pretending the pain never existed but rather surrendering it to God so that He can replace it with His peace and restoration.

2. Pray for Strength and Guidance Forgiveness can be challenging, and we cannot do it in our own strength. Lean on God through prayer, asking Him to give you the strength to forgive and the wisdom to take the right steps. When you bring your struggles before Him, He

will provide the grace and clarity you need to move forward.

James 1:5 reminds us, *"If any of you lacks wisdom, you should ask God, who gives generously to all without finding fault, and it will be given to you."* Ask God for wisdom in handling difficult emotions and situations, trusting that He will lead you on the right path.

Additionally, pray for healing in your heart. Unforgiveness can leave deep wounds, but God is the ultimate healer. Invite Him into your pain, and allow His love to restore and renew you. As you seek His guidance, He will give you peace and the strength to walk in true forgiveness.

3. Reflect on God's Forgiveness Take time to meditate on the countless times God has forgiven you, despite your mistakes and shortcomings. His grace is boundless, and His mercy is new every morning (Lamentations 3:22-23). When we remember how much we have been forgiven, it becomes easier to extend that same grace to others.

Ephesians 4:32 reminds us, *"Be kind and compassionate to one another, forgiving each other, just as in Christ God forgave you."* Just as God freely forgives us, He calls us to do the same for others.

Reflecting on God's forgiveness shifts our perspective. Instead of focusing on the pain someone has caused us, we are reminded of the undeserved grace we have received. Let this reflection soften your heart, strengthen your spirit, and inspire you to forgive as God has forgiven you.

4. Choose Forgiveness Forgiveness begins with a decision. It is not based on emotions or waiting until you "feel" ready but rather on a conscious choice to obey God's command to forgive. By choosing to forgive, we align ourselves with God's will and create a space for healing to occur.

Jesus teaches us the importance of this decision in **Matthew 6:14-15**, *"For if you forgive others their trespasses, your heavenly Father will also forgive you. But if you do not forgive others their trespasses, neither will your Father forgive your trespasses."*

Choosing forgiveness does not mean excusing the wrong or forgetting what happened—it means surrendering the burden to God and trusting Him to bring justice, healing, and peace. As you take this step in faith, trust that God will work on your heart, helping you walk in true freedom and grace.

5. Communicate, If Possible If it feels appropriate and safe, consider having an honest conversation with the person who hurt you. Open and respectful communication can bring clarity, foster understanding, and, in some cases, lead to reconciliation.

Matthew 18:15 encourages us, *"If your brother or sister sins, go and point out their fault, just between the two of you. If they listen to you, you have won them over."* Addressing issues with humility and grace can create an opportunity for healing and restoration.

Before initiating the conversation, pray for wisdom and a spirit of peace. Approach the discussion with a willingness to listen, not just to be heard. Remember, reconciliation is not always guaranteed, but honest communication can help you express your feelings, set healthy boundaries, and find closure.

Whether or not the relationship is restored, choosing to communicate with love and understanding reflects God's grace and brings peace to your own heart.

6. Pray for the Offender Praying for someone who has hurt you can be one of the most difficult steps in the forgiveness process, but it is also one of the most powerful. When we lift those who have wronged us up in prayer, we release bitterness and make room for God's healing work in our hearts.

Jesus teaches in **Matthew 5:44**, *"Love your enemies and pray for those who persecute you."* This instruction is not about ignoring the hurt but about surrendering it to God. Prayer softens our hearts, helping us see others through the lens of grace rather than resentment.

Start by asking God to help you forgive and bless the person who hurt you. It may feel unnatural at first, but as you continue to pray, your heart will begin to change. Over time, you will find yourself experiencing more peace, healing, and freedom as God's love works through you.

7. Seek Reconciliation When Possible Forgiveness and reconciliation are not always the same. While forgiveness is a personal choice to release resentment, reconciliation involves restoring a relationship—and this is not always possible or advisable. However, where it is safe and appropriate, seeking to mend broken relationships can bring healing and peace.

Romans 12:18 reminds us, *"If it is possible, as far as it depends on you, live at peace with everyone."* This verse acknowledges that reconciliation is a two-way process and may not always be achievable. Still, as followers of Christ, we are called to do our part in fostering peace and extending grace.

If reconciliation is possible, approach it with humility, patience, and wisdom. Open, honest communication, set healthy boundaries if needed, and allow God to guide the process. Whether or not reconciliation happens, choosing forgiveness ensures that your heart remains free from bitterness and open to God's love.

8. Set Healthy Boundaries Forgiveness does not mean tolerating harmful behavior or allowing others to continue hurting you. It is possible to forgive while also setting healthy boundaries to protect your emotional, mental, and spiritual well-being.

Proverbs 4:23 reminds us, *"Above all else, guard your heart, for everything you do flows from it."* Setting boundaries is a way to guard your heart while maintaining a spirit of grace and forgiveness.

Boundaries may include limiting contact with a person, clearly communicating your needs, or choosing how much access someone has to your life. These boundaries are not about punishment but about maintaining peace and ensuring that forgiveness does not come at the cost of your well-being.

Wisdom and forgiveness are inseparable. By setting healthy boundaries, you create space for healing, allowing yourself to move forward in love while protecting yourself from further harm.

9. Seek Support Forgiveness can be a difficult journey, and you don't have to walk it alone. Turn to trusted friends, family members, or a pastor for encouragement, prayer, and wise counsel. Sharing your struggles with

others can provide comfort, perspective, and clarity as you navigate the process of healing and letting go.

Proverbs 11:14 reminds us, *"Where there is no guidance, a people falls, but in an abundance of counselors there is safety."* Seeking support from those who are spiritually mature and compassionate can help you process your emotions and make wise decisions.

Surround yourself with people who will uplift you, remind you of God's truth, and encourage you to walk in faith. With the right support, forgiveness can become a tangible act of faith, allowing you to experience the peace and joy that come from living in harmony with God and others.

10. Trust God for Justice Forgiveness does not mean excusing or condoning wrongdoing. It means releasing the desire for revenge and trusting God to handle justice in His perfect way and timing. When we try to take matters into our own hands, we carry a burden that was never meant for us.

Romans 12:19 reminds us, *"Do not take revenge, my dear friends, but leave room for God's wrath, for it is written: 'It is mine to avenge; I will repay,' says the Lord."*

God is a just and righteous judge. He sees every wrong and promises to bring justice according to His wisdom. When we trust Him, we free ourselves from the exhausting cycle of bitterness and resentment. Instead of dwelling on the pain, we can rest in the assurance that God will make all things right in His time.

Letting go of the need for justice on our terms allows us to focus on healing, peace, and spiritual growth. Trust God's plan, and let Him handle what only He can.

11. Pray for Strength and Guidance Forgiveness can be challenging, and we cannot do it in our own strength. Lean on God through prayer, asking Him to give you the strength to forgive and the wisdom to take the right steps. When you bring your struggles before Him, He will provide the grace and clarity you need to move forward.

James 1:5 reminds us, *"If any of you lacks wisdom, you should ask God, who gives generously to all without finding fault, and it will be given to you."* Ask God for wisdom in handling difficult emotions and situations, trusting that He will lead you on the right path.

Additionally, pray for healing in your heart. Unforgiveness can leave deep wounds, but God is the ultimate healer. Invite Him into your pain, and allow His love to restore and renew you. As you seek His guidance, He will give you peace and the strength to walk in true forgiveness.

Encouragement to Embrace Forgiveness

Forgiveness is not a display of weakness; it is among the most courageous and liberating decisions we can make. It requires humility to let go of resentment, grace to extend mercy, and faith to trust in God's power to heal and restore. Choosing to forgive does not mean forgetting the pain, but rather surrendering it to God and allowing Him to bring peace to your heart.

As you walk through the journey of forgiveness, remember that you are never alone. God is with you, offering His strength and comfort every step of the way. He understands your pain and invites you to lean on Him as you choose to let go and move forward.

Let the words of **Colossians 3:13** inspire you: *"Bear with each other and forgive one another if any of you has a grievance against someone. Forgive as the Lord forgave you."*

By choosing forgiveness, you reflect the heart of God, embody His love, and unlock the path to peace, freedom, and spiritual growth. Consider what step you will take today to begin your journey toward true forgiveness.

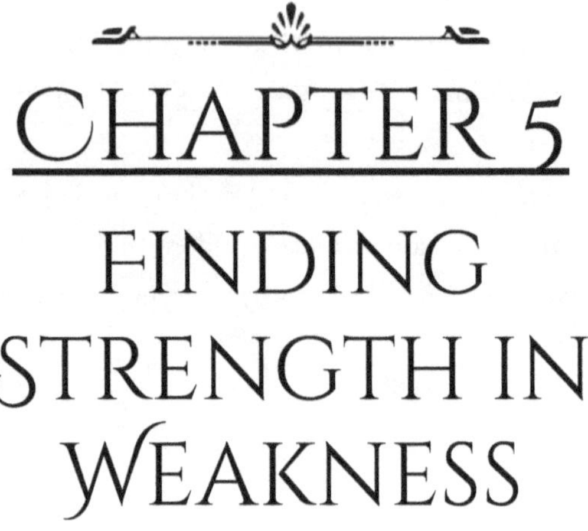

CHAPTER 5

FINDING STRENGTH IN WEAKNESS

Admitting weakness can feel like failure in a culture that values self-reliance, perfection, and power. In God's divine order, weakness is not a hindrance but an opportunity for His strength to shine. This chapter explores how God shows His greatness through our limitations. It shares inspiring stories of overcoming challenges and encourages you to embrace your imperfections as part of His plan.

We often view our weaknesses as obstacles—barriers that hinder us from realizing our full potential. But what if our weaknesses were not liabilities but rather opportunities for God to show His strength?

The **Apostle Paul**, in **2 Corinthians 12:9**, beautifully captures this truth:

"But he said to me, 'My grace is sufficient for you, for my power is made perfect in weakness.'"

This verse disrupts traditional views of strength, proposing that our limitations are not meant to weaken us but to serve as pathways for

God's divine power. **True strength is not found in self-sufficiency but in dependence on God.**

This humility allows Him to work, empowering us to surpass our human limitations. Instead of **concealing our flaws**, we are encouraged to **bring them before God**, trusting that **His grace is more than enough**. When we **hide our weaknesses**, we carry **unnecessary burdens**—trying to fix ourselves in our own strength. But God never asks for **perfection**—He asks for **honesty, surrender, and trust**.

Why Does God Want Us to Present Our Flaws to Him?

1. **It Deepens Our Dependence on Him**
   - When we acknowledge our weaknesses, we recognize our **need for God**. This draws us closer to Him, allowing His **strength to work in and through us**.
   - **2 Corinthians 12:9** reminds us: *"My grace is sufficient for you, for my power is made perfect in weakness."*
2. **It Frees Us from the Pressure to Be Perfect**
   - We often feel the need to **mask our flaws**, fearing judgment or failure. But when we surrender them to God, we experience **freedom from striving** and step into His **unconditional love and acceptance**.
   - **Psalm 55:22** encourages us: *"Cast your cares on the Lord and He will sustain you."*
3. **It Transforms Weakness into a Testimony**
   - What we see as **flaws, failures, or struggles**, God sees

as opportunities to **show His power and grace.**

- Just as He used **Moses' speech limitations, Gideon's fear, and Paul's hardships**, He can use **our weaknesses for His purpose.**

By **bringing our weaknesses to God**, we shift our focus from **our limitations to His unlimited power. His grace covers every shortcoming**, and His strength will **carry us where our own abilities cannot. Surrender today**, and watch how God transforms your weaknesses into a testimony of His strength.

What specific actions can you take to bring your weaknesses to God's attention? For instance, you can...

1. **Pray Honestly** – Talk to God openly about your struggles, fears, and weaknesses. **1 Peter 5:7** reminds us: *"Cast all your anxiety on Him because He cares for you."*

2. **Journal Your Weaknesses & God's Promises** – Write down the areas where you feel weak, and then find **Scriptures** that remind you of God's **strength and faithfulness.**

3. **Surrender Daily** – Each day, make a habit of saying, **"Lord, I give You my weaknesses. Work through me and help me trust in Your strength."**

4. **Seek Support** – Surround yourself with individuals who will pray for you, offer encouragement, and help you remember God's power.

By **bringing your weaknesses to God**, you shift the focus from **your limitations to His limitless power. His grace is more than sufficient, and He will utilize your weaknesses to fulfill His plan in your life.**

As we progress through this chapter, let's delve into real-life examples, biblical insights, and actionable steps that will facilitate our journey to finding strength in weakness and embracing God's grace.

How God Uses Our Weaknesses to Show His Strength

The **Apostle Paul's** words in **2 Corinthians 12:9** provide profound insight into the connection between **weakness and God's power**:

"But He said to me, 'My grace is sufficient for you, for my power is made perfect in weakness.' Therefore I will boast all the more gladly about my weaknesses, so that Christ's power may rest on me."

Paul understood that **his human frailties were not barriers to God's work** but rather **vessels for divine strength** to be revealed. When we embrace our limitations and recognize our need for God, we shift our focus from self-sufficiency to God's more than enough grace.

Why Does God Use Our Weaknesses?

1. **Weakness Leads to Dependence on God**
   When we acknowledge our weaknesses, we admit that we cannot rely solely on our own strength. This dependence **draws us closer to God** and allows His power to sustain us in ways we never imagined.

2. **Weakness Magnifies God's Glory**

If we were always strong, we might be tempted to take credit for our victories. But when God works through our **struggles and inadequacies**, His power becomes evident, and He receives the glory.

3. **Weakness Allows God to Transform Us**
Often, our greatest growth comes from our most challenging moments. God uses **brokenness, failure, and struggles** to refine our character, increase our faith, and equip us for His purpose.

Embracing Weakness as a Gift

Instead of seeing weakness as a limitation, we can see it as an opportunity to experience God's power in a deeper way. Just as Paul boasted in his weaknesses, we too can give our struggles to God, trusting that His grace will be enough for every challenge we face.

Surrendering Your Weaknesses to God

Which specific areas of **weakness** in your life can you surrender to God today? **Reflect on the challenges you face**, and allow Him to **transform them into sources of strength**, testifying to **His power and faithfulness.**

Here are some areas where you may be struggling:

- **Fear and Anxiety** – Do you find yourself overwhelmed with worry about the future? **Surrender your fears to God and trust in His perfect peace** (*Philippians 4:6-7*).

- **Doubt and Insecurity** – Are you questioning your worth

or abilities? **Allow God to remind you that you are fearfully and wonderfully made** (*Psalm 139:14*).

- **Past Mistakes and Regrets** – Are you holding onto guilt or shame? **Trust in God's forgiveness and grace, knowing that He makes all things new** (*2 Corinthians 5:17*).
- **Weakness in Faith** – Do you struggle to trust God fully? **Ask Him to strengthen your faith and help you rely on Him completely** (*Mark 9:24*).
- **Emotional Wounds and Brokenness** – Are you carrying past hurts? **Let God bring healing and restoration** (*Psalm 147:3*).
- **Physical Limitations or Health Struggles** – Are you battling sickness or exhaustion? **Rest in God's sustaining power and healing touch** (*Isaiah 40:29*).

God's promise remains true: His grace is sufficient, and His power is made perfect in weakness (*2 Corinthians 12:9*). Whatever burden you are carrying today, **place it in His hands**, and watch as He turns your **struggles into testimonies of His goodness and strength**.

What will you surrender to Him today?

God's Strength in Our Weakness: Biblical Examples

This truth is evident throughout Scripture—God chooses the weak and the unlikely to do His greatest works.

- **Moses** felt inadequate because of his speech impediment, but God called him to lead Israel out of slavery. Despite

Moses' objections, God reassured him, saying, *"I will help you speak and will teach you what to say"* (**Exodus 4:12**).

- **Gideon**, hiding in fear, saw himself as the weakest in his family. Yet, God called him to deliver Israel from the Midianites, declaring, *"The Lord is with you, mighty warrior"* (**Judges 6:12**). God saw **not who Gideon was, but who he could become** through His strength.

- **David**, a young shepherd, faced the giant **Goliath** with only a sling and five stones. While others saw an **impossible battle**, David trusted in **God's power**, proving that **victory belongs to the Lord** (**1 Samuel 17**).

In each of these cases, God used **ordinary, flawed individuals** to accomplish **extraordinary** things. Their weaknesses became opportunities for God's power to be revealed. **The same is true for you**—your limitations are not barriers; they are invitations for God to work through you in ways you never imagined.

Where do you feel weak today? Take a moment to reflect on areas where you may need God's strength and guidance. Trust that God can turn your greatest struggles into powerful testimonies of His grace.

Stories of Individuals Who Turned Their Struggles into Testimonies

1. Nick Vujicic: Living Without Limits Nick Vujicic was born with **tetra-amelia syndrome (**Vujicic, 2010), a rare disorder characterized by the absence of all four limbs. Facing immense challenges from an early age, he battled feelings of hopelessness, bullying, and even thoughts of suicide. Yet, rather than allowing his physical condition to define him, he embraced **God's greater purpose** for his life.

Through faith, perseverance, and a deep trust in God's plan, **Nick transformed his struggles into a powerful testimony of hope and resilience** (Vujicic, 2012). He became a globally renowned **motivational speaker, evangelist, and author**, sharing his journey with millions. His message emphasizes that no obstacle is too great when faith is at the center, often citing **Matthew 19:26**: *"With God all things are possible."*

Today, **Nick Vujicic travels the world**, inspiring others to overcome their challenges, trust in God's plan, and embrace life without limits. His story is a testament to how **God's strength is made perfect in weakness** (2 Corinthians 12:9), proving that our limitations can become the very platforms that God uses for His glory.

2. Corrie ten Boom: Forgiveness After Betrayal Corrie ten Boom, a Dutch Christian watchmaker, and her family risked their lives during **World War II** by sheltering Jews from the Nazis (ten Boom & Sherrill, 1971). Their courageous efforts were discovered, leading to their **arrest and imprisonment** in the **Ravensbrück concentration camp**. Corrie suffered immense loss—her father died shortly after being arrested, and her beloved sister **Betsie** perished in the camp.

Despite enduring **unimaginable suffering**, Corrie clung to her **faith in God**, finding strength in His promises. After the war, she became an international speaker, sharing her story of **forgiveness and redemption**. One of her most profound moments came when she **forgave one of the former guards from Ravensbrück**, demonstrating **God's transformative power**. She famously stated,

Corrie's life is a testament to **God's ability to bring beauty from brokenness**. She believed that **forgiveness is not an option but a command**, drawing from **Matthew 6:14-15**, which teaches that our willingness to forgive others is deeply connected to receiving God's forgiveness.

Through her powerful testimony, **Corrie ten Boom showed the world that faith can triumph over hate, love can heal the deepest wounds, and forgiveness is the path to true freedom**.

3. Bethany Hamilton: Faith on the Waves At just 13 years old, **Bethany Hamilton** faced a life-altering tragedy when a **14-foot tiger shark** attacked her while she was surfing off the coast of Hawaii, resulting in the loss of her left arm (Hamilton, 2004). For many, such an event would have marked the end of their dreams—but for Bethany, it became the beginning of an **extraordinary testimony of faith and resilience**.

Rather than giving in to fear or discouragement, Bethany **leaned on her unwavering faith in God**. Just one month after the attack, she was back in the ocean, determined to surf again. Through perseverance and trust in God's plan, she not only adapted to her new reality but went on to become a **professional surfer**, inspiring millions worldwide with her courage.

Bethany's journey reflects the promise of **Isaiah 40:31**:

"But those who hope in the Lord will renew their strength. They will soar on wings like eagles; they will run and not grow weary, they will walk and not be faint."

Her story is a powerful reminder that even in the face of life's greatest setbacks, faith can sustain us. Bethany has since shared her testimony through books, films, and speaking engagements, encouraging others to trust in **God's strength over their limitations** (Hamilton, 2014).

4. Joni Eareckson Tada: Finding Purpose in Paralysis At just 17 years old, **Joni Eareckson Tada** suffered a **diving accident** that left her paralyzed from the shoulders down (Tada, 2006). Facing the reality of living as a quadriplegic, she experienced deep **despair, anger, and doubt**. However, through her **faith in Christ**, she found renewed purpose, turning her suffering into a **powerful testimony of perseverance and hope**.

Instead of allowing her disability to define her, Joni used her circumstances to **inspire millions**. She became an **author, speaker, and advocate for people with disabilities**, proving that **God's power is made perfect in weakness (2 Corinthians 12:9)**. Through her organization, **Joni and Friends**, she has ministered to thousands, providing **wheelchairs, resources, and spiritual encouragement** to those in need (Tada, 2010).

Joni's story reminds us that **no struggle is too great for God to use for His glory**. As she once said,

Her journey is a **living testament** to the truth that even in suffering, God can **bring beauty, healing, and a greater purpose**.

5. Wilma Rudolph: Overcoming Adversity to Become an Olympic Champion Born prematurely at **4.5 pounds**, Wilma Rudolph suffered from **polio, scarlet fever, and pneumonia** as a child, leaving her **unable to walk properly** for much of her early life (Rudolph, 1977). Doctors doubted she would ever walk again, yet through **determination, faith, and support from her family**, Wilma defied all odds.

By age 12, she had **regained her ability to walk**. Through years of **hard work and perseverance**, she not only walked but **became one of the fastest women in the world**. At the **1960 Olympic Games**, Wilma won **three gold medals**, becoming the **first American woman to achieve such a feat in track and field** (Pinkney, 2000).

Her story echoes the biblical promise of **Philippians 4:13**:

"I can do all things through Christ who strengthens me."

Wilma's **faith, resilience, and unwavering spirit** remind us that **God can turn our greatest struggles into our most powerful victories.**

6. C.S. Lewis: Finding Faith Through Suffering C.S. Lewis, one of the most **influential Christian writers and theologians**, was once an **atheist** who struggled deeply with the **problem of suffering** (Lewis, 1940). After losing his mother at a young age, experiencing the horrors of **World War I**, and later enduring the painful loss of his wife, Lewis wrestled with **doubt, grief, and faith**.

Yet, through his suffering, he discovered **a profound trust in God**. His experiences led him to write **some of the most powerful Christian literature**, including *Mere Christianity* and *The Problem of Pain*, which help believers **understand faith in the midst of hardship** (Lewis, 1952).

Lewis once wrote,

His testimony reminds us that **faith is not about the absence of struggle but about trusting God through it**.

God's Power in Our Weakness: Biblical Examples

Countless individuals throughout **biblical history** have experienced **God's transformative power** in the midst of their weaknesses. Seemingly insurmountable challenges transformed into compelling testimonies of God's strength manifesting through human weakness.

- *"Pardon your servant, Lord. I have never been eloquent, neither in the past nor since you have spoken to your servant. I am slow of speech and tongue."* **(Exodus 4:10, NIV)***"Now go; I will help you speak and will teach you what to say."* **(Exodus 4:12, NIV)Moses: Called Despite His Weakness:** A **stutterer** called to **lead a nation**? By human standards, Moses was an unlikely choice for such a monumental task. When God called him to **lead the Israelites out of Egypt**, Moses doubted his own abilities, saying:

Yet, God's response was clear:

- *"You come against me with sword and spear and javelin, but I come against you in the name of the Lord Almighty, the God of the armies of Israel, whom you have defied."* **(1 Samuel 17:45, NIV)David: A Shepherd Boy Turned Giant Slayer:** A **shepherd boy** facing a **formidable giant**? David appeared to be an improbable champion. He was **young, inexperienced**, and **armed only with a sling and five stones**, while Goliath stood as a battle-hardened warrior with overwhelming strength. Yet, David's victory was not about his size, skill, or weaponry—it was about his **unwavering faith in God**.

When David confronted Goliath, he declared:

- *"But He said to me, 'My grace is sufficient for you, for my power is made perfect in weakness.' Therefore I will boast all the more gladly about my weaknesses, so that Christ's power may rest on me."* (**2 Corinthians 12:9, NIV**)**The Apostle Paul: Strength Through Suffering:** Persecuted, **imprisoned, beaten, shipwrecked, and facing countless hardships, Paul's weaknesses** did not hinder his mission—they became the very **platform for God's extraordinary grace** to shine through.

Despite his suffering, Paul declared:

These stories—and countless others—demonstrate that **our weaknesses are not barriers to God's purpose** but rather **opportunities for Him to shine**. When we surrender our limitations to Him, He turns them into instruments of **strength, victory, and transformation**.

God chooses the **unlikely**, empowers the **weak**, and works through **brokenness** to reveal **His glory**. As **2 Corinthians 12:9** reminds us:

No matter your struggles, insecurities, or perceived shortcomings, **God can use you** in ways beyond your imagination. **Will you trust Him to turn your weakness into a testimony of His strength? The choice is yours.**

Our culture often pressures us to **hide our flaws** and present a **polished, perfect version of ourselves**. However, God's Word teaches that our imperfections are not liabilities, but rather the very places where His power is most evident. Rather than seeing weaknesses as obstacles, we can embrace them as **opportunities for God's grace to work in us and through us**.

1. God's Strength Is Sufficient No matter your struggle—**physical limitations, past mistakes, emotional wounds, or personal insecurities—God's grace is always enough**. He does not require perfection; He simply calls for **a willing heart that trusts in Him**.

Romans 8:28 assures us:

This promise reminds us that **God is not limited by our limitations.** Where we see **weakness**, He sees **possibility**. Where we feel **insufficient**, He proves **His sufficiency**. He can use **every broken piece** of our lives to bring about **His divine purpose**.

Instead of striving for **worldly perfection**, let us embrace the truth that **God's power is made perfect in our weakness** (**2 Corinthians 12:9**). When we surrender our flaws to Him, we step into **true freedom**, knowing that **He is the one who perfects us in His strength**.

2. Weakness Invites Dependency on God When we **acknowledge our weaknesses**, we create space for **God's strength** to work in and through us. Rather than viewing our limitations as failures, we can see them as **invitations to rely on God's power** rather than our own.

Psalm 46:1 reminds us:

When we try to navigate life in **our own strength**, we often feel exhausted, discouraged, and overwhelmed. But when we **depend on**

God, we experience **His supernatural power** in ways we never could on our own. His strength **sustains us in difficulties, uplifts us in struggles, and empowers us in our calling**.

Just as a child **depends on a loving parent** for guidance and protection, we are called to **lean on God with full trust and confidence**. Weakness is not a sign of defeat—it is an opportunity to experience **God's sufficiency** in every aspect of our lives. When we let go of **self-reliance**, we can fully embrace **God's limitless strength**.

3. Your Story Has a Purpose Your struggles are not meaningless—they are a **part of your testimony**. Every hardship, setback, and trial you have faced is an opportunity for **God's glory to be revealed**. When you allow Him to work through your challenges, He can use your story to **inspire, uplift, and encourage others**.

Revelation 12:11 declares:

This verse reminds us that **our testimonies have power**. By sharing how God has **brought you through difficulties, healed your wounds, or strengthened you in weakness**, you give others **hope and faith** that He can do the same for them.

Your journey—**with all its ups and downs**—is part of **God's greater purpose**. Instead of hiding your struggles, embrace them as a **testament to His faithfulness**. Someone out there needs to hear your story to be reminded that **God is still working, still healing, and still restoring lives**.

What specific part of your story can you share today to point others toward God's grace and strength? Consider sharing about a time when...

Embrace Your Imperfections and Trust in God's Strength

Embrace your imperfections, acknowledge your limitations, and recognize your dependence on God. By doing so, you pave the way for the manifestation of miracles, transformation, and divine purpose in your life.

- *"Therefore confess your sins to each other and pray for each other so that you may be healed. The prayer of a righteous person is powerful and effective."* **(NIV)Embrace vulnerability:** Don't be afraid to **share your struggles with others**. Vulnerability is not weakness—it is a gateway to **authentic connection** and an opportunity for **God to work through you**. When you open your heart, you invite others to see **God's power at work in your life**.

James 5:16
reminds us:

- *"I can do all things through Christ who strengthens me."* **Seek God's strength:** Rather than relying on your own strength, **turn to God's limitless power**. When faced with challenges, lean on His **grace, wisdom, and provision**. **Philippians 4:13** assures us:

No matter what you are facing,
God's strength is sufficient
to carry you through.

- *"My grace is sufficient for you, for my power is made perfect in weakness."* **Celebrate your weaknesses:** Instead of seeing your weaknesses as **flaws**, view them as **opportunities for God to reveal His power**. **2 Corinthians 12:9** reminds us:

When you embrace your weaknesses, you allow
God to shape, refine, and transform you
into the person He created you to be.

Your Worth is Found in God, Not in Perfection: Your weaknesses do not define your worth. They are simply places where God's extraordinary power and grace can shine. Embrace your imperfections, trust in His plan, and watch as He transforms your weaknesses into strengths—for His glory and your good.

Remember, **your weaknesses are not a measure of your worth**. They do not diminish your value or disqualify you from God's purpose. Instead, they are **opportunities for God to reveal His extraordinary power and grace** in your life.

2 Corinthians 12:9 reminds us:

When you **embrace your imperfections**, you invite God to **work through you** in ways you never imagined. Your struggles, flaws, and limitations are not obstacles, but rather the very places where God's strength can be most evident.

Trust in Him, surrender your weaknesses, and watch as **He transforms them into strengths**—not for your glory, but for His. **You**

are not defined by your shortcomings but by the limitless power of the God who works through them.

Practical Steps to Find Strength in Weakness

Here are some ways to **embrace your imperfections** and allow **God's strength** to work in your life:

1. Surrender Your Struggles Take your **weaknesses, fears, and doubts** to God in **prayer**. Be honest about your **struggles and limitations**, and invite Him to work **through them** rather than against them. When you surrender to Him, you allow His **peace and power** to sustain you.

Philippians 4:6-7 reminds us:

Instead of **struggling alone**, trust that **God is in control**. Lay down your burdens and **rest in His perfect peace. He is more than capable of turning your weaknesses into strengths**—all He asks is that you bring them to Him.

2. Meditate on God's Promises When you feel **inadequate or discouraged, remind yourself of God's promises**. His Word is filled with **assurances of His presence, strength, and faithfulness**. Meditating on Scripture renews your **mind, strengthens your faith**, and shifts your **perspective from weakness to trust in His power**.

Two powerful verses to hold onto are:

- **2 Corinthians 12:9—"My** *grace is sufficient for you, for my power is made perfect in weakness."* **(NIV)**

    - This verse reminds us that **God's grace is always**

enough, even when we feel weak or unqualified.

- **Isaiah 41:10**—"Do *not fear, for I am with you; do not be dismayed, for I am your God. I will strengthen you and help you; I will uphold you with my righteous right hand."* (**NIV**)
    - God promises to **strengthen and uphold** us, no matter what challenges we face.

Practical Tip: Write down **key Bible verses** that encourage you and place them **where you can see them daily**—on your mirror, in your journal, or as phone reminders. When doubt creeps in, **speak God's promises over your life** and **trust that He is always with you.**

3. Take One Step of Faith at a Time Don't wait until you feel **"ready" or "perfect"** to step into what God has called you to do. **Perfection is not a requirement for obedience—faith is.** God doesn't expect you to have everything figured out; He simply asks you to **trust Him and take the next step.**

Hebrews 11:1 reminds us:

Walking in faith means **trusting God even when the path ahead is uncertain. Moses, David, Esther, and Peter**—none of them had all the answers when they stepped forward in obedience, but God **equipped them as they moved forward.**

Practical Tip: Identify one small step you can take today toward what God is calling you to do.

- Pray for **courage and trust**, knowing that **God goes before you.**
- Remember, **faith grows as you walk in it**—God will equip you as you take each step forward.

What step of faith can you take today? Trust that **God is already preparing the way** for you.

4. Seek Community Surround yourself with **people who uplift you, encourage you, and point you back to God**. We were never meant to **walk this journey of faith alone**—God designed us for **community and support**. When we face challenges, having a **strong, faith-filled community** helps us **stay encouraged and keep moving forward.**

Ecclesiastes 4:9-10 reminds us:

Why is community important?

- Encouragement: **When you feel weak, others can remind you of God's faithfulness.**
- Accountability: **A strong community will challenge and strengthen your faith.**
- Prayer Support: **Having others pray for you brings strength and comfort.**

Practical Tip:

- **Find a Bible study group, church community, or mentor** who will encourage and support your faith.
- **Be intentional about building godly relationships** that help you grow spiritually.
- **Don't be afraid to ask for help**—God often speaks through the wisdom and encouragement of others.

Who in your life can you lean on for encouragement today? If you don't have a strong faith community, **pray for God to bring the right people into your life.**

5. Share Your Story Your **testimony** has the power to **inspire, encourage, and bring hope to others**. When you **share how God has worked in your life**, even through struggles, you become a **living example of His faithfulness. Your story is a testimony of God's grace**—it shows that He can transform **weakness into strength, pain into purpose, and trials into triumphs**.

Revelation 12:11 declares:

When you **open up about your journey**, you remind others that **they are not alone** and that **God is still in the business of redemption and transformation**.

Practical Tip:

- **Write down your testimony**—how has God helped you through struggles?

- **Share it with someone who needs encouragement**, whether in person, through social media, or in a small group.
- **Remember, vulnerability is powerful**—you don't need a perfect story; you just need a willing heart to share **God's goodness**.

Who in your life could benefit from your story today? Don't be afraid to share—it may be exactly what someone needs to hear to **find faith, hope, and strength in their own journey.**

A Final Word of Encouragement

God delights in using the broken, the flawed, and the imperfect to accomplish His purposes. Your weaknesses are not a mistake—they are part of His divine plan to **reveal His power and display His glory** through your life.

By embracing your imperfections and trusting in His strength, you will realize that His grace surpasses all, and His power is truly perfected in weakness (2 Corinthians 12:9).

Take heart in these words from **Isaiah 40:29**:

No matter what struggles, doubts, or limitations you face, **God's strength is always sufficient**. Your weaknesses don't limit him; he overcomes them.

Be encouraged. God is ready to work **powerfully in and through your life. Which weakness will you surrender to Him**

today? Entrust it to His care, and witness the transformation into a testament of His strength, grace, and faithfulness.

CHAPTER 6

FACING UNCERTAINTY WITH FAITH

Life is like a winding road, with unexpected twists and turns that can make you feel uncertain and apprehensive about the future. Whether it's an **unexpected career change, a health crisis, or waiting for clarity on a major decision**, uncertainty can leave us feeling **vulnerable, anxious, and unsettled**. Yet, these moments are **not without purpose**—they are invitations to **deepen our trust in God**.

Faith is not the absence of uncertainty but the confidence to move forward despite unclear paths. True faith is rooted in trusting God, not in having all the answers. **Proverbs 3:5-6** encourages us:

Navigating Uncertainty with Faith: Strategies for Trusting God in Uncertain Times

Life is rarely a **predictable, linear journey**. We often find ourselves **navigating through seasons of uncertainty**, where the path ahead is shrouded in mist, and doubt creeps in. These times can be challenging, yet they also serve as valuable opportunities for spiritual growth.

Why? Because it is precisely in these moments that our **faith is tested, refined, and strengthened**. Just as a ship **relies on its anchor in stormy seas**, we are called to **anchor ourselves in God's promises**. He is our firm foundation, our unshakable hope, and our constant guide.

Embracing Uncertainty with Faith

Rather than allowing uncertainty to **paralyze us with fear**, we can choose to:

1. **Trust in God's Timing.** He sees the full picture, even when we don't, and guides us toward His perfect plan.

2. **Seek His Guidance**—Through prayer and His Word, we can find direction.

3. **Surrender Control**—Faith means releasing our need to have all the answers.

4. **Walk in Obedience**—Taking small steps forward, even when the outcome is unknown.

As we journey through this chapter, we will explore **how to navigate uncertainty with faith**, leaning on **God's promises and His**

unwavering presence. No matter how uncertain the road ahead may seem, God is already there, guiding your steps.

Navigating Uncertainty with Faith: Strategies for Trusting God in Uncertain Times

Faith often requires us to **step into the unknown**, trusting in **God's promises rather than our limited sight**. When we face uncertainty, it can be tempting to rely on **our own understanding**, searching for answers and control. Yet, the Bible calls us to **place our trust fully in God**, knowing that **His plans far exceed our comprehension**.

Proverbs 3:5-6 reminds us:

Faith is About Trust, Not Control

True faith is **not about having all the answers** or being in perfect control. It is about **trusting in a God who is greater than our circumstances**, a God whose **plans and purposes** extend beyond our **human understanding**.

This verse emphasizes the importance of:

- **Surrendering our anxieties**—letting go of the need to **figure everything out** on our own.

- **Acknowledging God in all things**—seeking **His wisdom, presence, and direction** in every situation.

- **Trusting in His divine guidance**—believing that even

when the road ahead is uncertain, **God is leading us in the right direction**.

Walking by Faith, Not by Sight

Walking by Faith, Not by Sight

Faith does not mean we will always see the path clearly before us—it means trusting that **God is guiding each step**, even when we don't fully understand where it leads. **Isaiah 55:8-9** reminds us:

If you are facing a **season of uncertainty**, take heart: **God sees the full picture, and He is leading you with purpose and love. Will you trust Him, even when the path isn't clear?**

Building Trust Through Uncertainty: Strengthening Your Faith Amid Challenges

Trusting God **does not mean ignoring challenges** or pretending that uncertainty isn't difficult. Instead, it means **surrendering our desire for control** and choosing to believe that **God is sovereign, good, and always at work**—even when we can't see the full picture.

When life feels uncertain, we have a choice: **will we rely on our own understanding, or will we trust in God's perfect plan?**

1. Acknowledge God's Sovereignty

God sees what we cannot. **He knows the past, present, and future**, and His wisdom surpasses our own. When we trust in His sovereignty, we recognize that **His plans are greater than ours**.

Isaiah 55:8-9 reminds us:

Even when life seems uncertain, **God is in control, and His plan always unfolds with purpose and precision**.

2. Rely on His Character

Our trust in God grows when we **remember who He is—faithful, loving, and unchanging**. Unlike people and circumstances that shift, **God remains constant**.

Hebrews 13:8 assures us:

When doubt creeps in, **reflect on God's past faithfulness** in your life. If He has been faithful before, **He will be faithful again**.

3. Embrace His Timing

One of the greatest struggles in uncertainty is **impatience**—wanting answers **now**. But God operates on **a perfect timeline**, shaping events in ways we cannot yet understand.

Ecclesiastes 3:11 encourages us:

Waiting is never easy, but **God's timing is always perfect**. Even when delays seem like setbacks, they are often **divine preparations** for something greater.

Choosing Faith Over Fear

Uncertainty may challenge us, but it also **deepens our faith**. **Trusting God in uncertainty** is **resting in His sovereignty, character, and perfect timing**.

What area of your life feels uncertain today? **Surrender it to God, knowing that He is in control, and trust that His plan is unfolding perfectly, even when you cannot see the full picture.**

Lessons from the Israelites' Journey Through the Wilderness

The **Israelites' journey** from **Egypt to the Promised Land** serves as a powerful lesson in **faith amid uncertainty**. What was meant to be an **11-day journey** stretched into **40 years**—not because **God failed them**, but because **they struggled to fully trust Him**.

Their experiences mirror our own: in seasons of **waiting, uncertainty, and hardship**, we are often tempted to **doubt God's faithfulness**. Yet, through their journey, we can learn valuable lessons about **trusting God in the unknown**.

1. Trusting God's Provision

When the Israelites **faced hunger and thirst**, instead of trusting God, **they grumbled** and questioned His ability to sustain them. Yet, despite their doubts, **God remained faithful**—providing **manna from heaven and water from a rock**.

Exodus "16:4—"Then *the Lord said to Moses, 'I will rain down bread from heaven for you.'"*

Exodus "17:6—"Strike *the rock, and water will come out of it for the people to drink."*

Lesson: In times of uncertainty, trust that God will meet your needs.

No matter what you are lacking—**provision, strength, guidance, or peace**—God is able to supply it. He does not lead His people into the wilderness **only to abandon them**.

Philippians 4:19 assures us:

Rather than worrying about what we lack, we can find peace in knowing that God provides for us. Even when resources seem scarce, His **grace is sufficient**, and His provision is **always on time**.

Are you trusting God's provision in your season of uncertainty?

Rather than **grumbling or fearing the unknown**, choose to **trust that He will supply everything you need—one day at a time.**

2. Following God's Guidance

During their journey, the **Israelites were not left to wander aimlessly**—God provided **clear guidance** through a **pillar of cloud by day** and a **pillar of fire by night**. His presence **never left them**, even when the path seemed uncertain.

Exodus 13:21-22 says:

Even though the **Israelites could see God's presence leading them**, they still doubted **His direction and timing**. They often questioned **why the journey was taking so long** or **why they had to go through the wilderness at all**. Yet, God's plan was **not just to get them to the Promised Land but to transform them along the way**.

Lesson: Trust God's Guidance, Even When It Doesn't Make Sense

God's leading in our lives may not always be **obvious or immediate**, but **His presence is constant**. When we don't understand **why we are in a difficult season or why we feel uncertain about the next step**, we can hold onto the truth that **God is still guiding us, even when we can't see the full picture.**

Psalm 119:105 reminds us:

God's Word is our **guiding light** in seasons of uncertainty. Even if He doesn't reveal the **entire path at once**, He gives us enough **light for the next step**.

Are You Trusting God's Leading?

When you feel lost or uncertain, lean on His presence. Seek His guidance through prayer and Scripture. Trust that He is leading you step by step. **Even when the journey feels slow, God is still working.**

3. Overcoming Doubt: The Impact of Uncertainty on Faith

Throughout their journey, the **Israelites faced many obstacles**, including **the Red Sea, scarcity of food and water, and eventually, the giants in the Promised Land**. Instead of holding onto faith in God's promises, they **allowed fear to overshadow their faith**.

One of the most defining moments of their journey occurred when Moses sent **twelve spies** to scout the **Promised Land (Numbers 13-14)**. Though the land was **rich and abundant**, ten of the spies focused on the **giants and fortified cities**, spreading fear among the people. Instead of trusting **God's power to deliver them**, the Israelites chose **doubt over faith**, which led to **forty years of wandering in the wilderness** instead of immediately stepping into their destiny.

Numbers 14:11 captures God's response:

Lesson: Fear Can Paralyze, but Faith Propels Us Forward

Doubt **delayed their destiny**. Instead of entering the **land God had promised**, their **fear led to disobedience**, causing an entire generation to miss out on **God's blessings**.

Fear often **magnifies obstacles and minimizes God's power**. It causes us to see problems as **bigger than God's promises**. But faith enables us to **move forward**, even when the path ahead seems intimidating.

Isaiah 41:10 encourages us:

Are You Allowing Fear to Hold You Back?

- **What "giants" are you facing in your life right now?**
- **Are you allowing fear to stop you from stepping into God's promises?**

Instead of **letting doubt delay your destiny, choose faith. Trust that God is greater than any obstacle**, and step forward, believing that **He will make a way where there seems to be none**. When you have faith, you will see miracles happen.

Lessons from the Israelites' Journey Through the Wilderness

The **Israelites' journey** through the wilderness powerfully illustrates **the challenges and rewards of trusting God in the face of uncertainty**. Their story mirrors our own faith journeys, in which we often struggle with **doubt, impatience, and fear**, yet God remains **faithful, guiding us toward His promises**.

1. God's Detours Provide Protection and Preparation

Exodus 13:17 explains why God led the Israelites on a longer path rather than the shorter, more direct route:

At first, this **detour** may have seemed **unnecessary** and **inconvenient**, but it was actually **an act of divine protection**. God **knew their fears and weaknesses**, and He guided them along the **path that would best prepare them for the Promised Land**.

Lesson: Sometimes, God's longer route is His way of protecting and preparing us.

When life doesn't go as planned, it's easy to question **why God isn't leading us on the quickest path**. But His **wisdom surpasses our**

understanding. What seems like a **delay** is often His **divine protection and preparation**.

2. Consequences of Complaining and Doubt

Despite experiencing **God's miracles**, the Israelites often **doubted and complained** in moments of difficulty. When they lacked food, they quickly forgot God's past faithfulness and **longed for Egypt**—the very place of their oppression.

Exodus 16:3 captures their frustration:

God responded **not with anger but with provision**, sending **manna from heaven and quail for them to eat**. Yet, their **continued grumbling revealed a lack of trust**.

Lesson: Grumbling blinds us to God's faithfulness.

In our own lives, when we focus on **what's missing**, we fail to see **what God is providing**. Instead of complaining, we are called to **trust and be grateful, even in seasons of hardship**.

3. Spiritual Growth in the Wilderness

God **did not lead the Israelites through the wilderness to punish them**, but rather to **test, humble, and refine them**.

Deuteronomy 8:2 explains the purpose of this journey:

The wilderness was not just about **reaching the destination**—it was about **preparing the people for what lay ahead**. It was a time of:

- Humbling—Teaching them to depend fully on God.
- Testing—Revealing the true condition of their hearts.
- Training—Strengthening their faith for the challenges to come.

Lesson: God uses seasons of uncertainty to refine our faith.

Difficult seasons are **not without purpose**. Just as the wilderness taught the Israelites to **rely on God for daily provision**, our own struggles teach us **to trust in His timing, strength, and faithfulness.**

Reflect on Your Trust in God During Uncertain Times: Where Do You Stand?

Life's **unexpected detours** can be discouraging, leaving us questioning why God isn't leading us on a **quicker, easier path**. But The wilderness is not the end of your journey; it is the place where you are refined for the promises that lie ahead.

Take a moment to reflect:

- **Do you feel like you're on a detour, wondering why God**

isn't taking you on a shorter path?

  - God's **delays are not denials**—sometimes, the longer route is **His way of preparing and protecting you**.

- **Are you tempted to grumble and doubt, forgetting His past faithfulness?**
  - Just as God provided **manna in the wilderness**, He is **providing for you now**—even if it looks different than expected.
- **Can you recognize this season as a time of spiritual growth, rather than just a trial?**
  - The wilderness is a place where faith is fortified, character is honed, and trust in God is deepened.

God Is Leading You, Even When the Path Feels Uncertain

Trust that **God is leading you, providing for you, and preparing you**—even when the journey feels long and unclear. **Keep walking in faith. The Promised Land is ahead.**

Strengthening Trust Through Prayer and Scripture Reflection

Faith **does not grow passively**—it requires **intentional seeking of God**, especially in **seasons of uncertainty**. Prayer and meditation on His Word are powerful ways to **strengthen our trust in Him**.

1. Prayer: Aligning Your Heart with God

Prayer is more than just **bringing our requests to God**; it is about **aligning our hearts with His will**. When we pray, we **invite God's presence into our situation**, allowing Him to replace **fear with faith and anxiety with peace**.

Philippians 4:6-7 encourages us:

Practical Ways to Strengthen Your Trust Through Prayer

- **Be Honest:**
  - Share your **fears, doubts, and uncertainties** with God.
  - He welcomes **honest prayers** and offers **comfort and reassurance**. **(Psalm 62:8)**
- **Listen:**
  - Prayer is a **two-way conversation**.
  - Spend time in **silence**, allowing God to **speak to your heart** through His Holy Spirit. **(John 10:27)**

- **Intercede for Others:**
    - Shift your focus from **worry to worship** by praying for others.
    - Trust that God is working **not only in your life** but in **every situation** around you. **(James 5:16)**

By committing to **consistent, heartfelt prayer**, you develop **a deeper trust in God's sovereignty**, even when life feels uncertain.

How Can You Start Today?

- Take **a few moments to pray**, bringing your uncertainties to God.
- Ask Him to **replace your fears with His peace**.
- Spend time in **silence, listening for His guidance**.

As you **seek Him daily**, you will find that **your trust in Him grows stronger**, and His **peace will guard your heart and mind, no matter what you face.**

2. Meditate on God's Word

God's Word is a source of truth, strength, and encouragement—especially in seasons of uncertainty. When we **meditate on Scripture**, we remind ourselves of **God's promises**, shifting our focus from **fear to faith. His Word renews our minds, strengthens our hearts, and equips us to face the unknown with confidence.**

Psalm 119:105 declares:

Even when we **don't see the full picture**, God's Word provides **the guidance we need to take the next step**.

Practical Ways to Meditate on Scripture:

- **Memorize Key Verses**
    - Store God's promises in your heart so they can **guide and comfort you in difficult moments**.
    - Verses like:
        - **Psalm 23**—Assurance of God's provision and protection.
        - **Romans 8:28**—Confidence that **God is working all things for good**.
        - **Matthew 6:25-34**—a reminder to **trust God instead of worrying about the future**.
- **Journal Your Reflections**
    - Write about **how God's Word applies to your current situation**.
    - Documenting **your thoughts, prayers, and insights** can help clarify **what God is teaching you**.
- **Declare His Promises Aloud**

  - **Speak God's Word over your life**, affirming your trust in His faithfulness.
  - *"Faith comes from hearing, and hearing through the word of Christ."* (**NIV**)**Romans 10:17** reminds us:
  - Declaring Scripture **builds faith**, reminds us of **God's character**, and strengthens our trust in Him.

How Can You Start Today?

- Choose **one verse** that speaks to your **current struggles** and **meditate on it throughout the day**.
- As a declaration of faith, write it down, memorize it, and speak it out loud.
- Allow **God's Word to fill your heart**, replacing fear with confidence in **His perfect plan**.

By immersing yourself in **Scripture daily**, you will find **peace, direction, and unshakable trust**—no matter how uncertain the road ahead may seem.

3. Cultivate Gratitude

Gratitude shifts our focus from what we lack to the blessings God has already bestowed upon us. When we practice gratitude, we **acknowledge God's faithfulness** in our past and trust Him for our future. It changes our perspective, helping us **see abundance rather than scarcity, blessings rather than burdens**.

1 Thessalonians 5:18 encourages us:

Even in **seasons of uncertainty**, **giving thanks** reminds us that **God is always at work, providing, guiding, and sustaining us**. Gratitude **strengthens our faith** and deepens our trust in **His ongoing provision**.

Practical Ways to Cultivate Gratitude

Gratitude **shifts our focus** from **what we lack** to **what God has already done**. By developing a habit of gratitude, we train our hearts to **see God's faithfulness**, even in difficult moments. Here are some practical ways to **cultivate gratitude daily**:

- **Keep a Gratitude Journal**
    - Write down **three things you are grateful for each day**, even in challenging seasons.
    - Reflecting on **past blessings** reminds you of **God's faithfulness** and strengthens your trust in Him.
    - When facing uncertainty, looking back at **how God has provided** can bring peace and confidence in His plans.
- *"Enter His gates with thanksgiving and His courts with praise; give thanks to Him and praise His name."* **(NIV)Thank God in Prayer**
    - Instead of focusing only on **requests**, begin prayers with

thanksgiving.

  - Express gratitude for **His love, provision, guidance, and faithfulness**.
  - **Psalm 100:4** reminds us:

- **Start Today: Speak Gratitude Aloud**
  - Declare **God's goodness over your life**, even when circumstances feel uncertain.
  - Verbally thanking God **shifts your mindset** from **worry to trust**.
  - Speaking His promises aloud **reinforces faith** and helps you focus on **His sovereignty rather than your struggles**.
  - Take a moment to **thank God right now**—whether in prayer, writing, or speaking out loud.
  - Make gratitude a **daily habit**, and watch how it transforms your **heart, perspective, and faith**.

We are **not meant to navigate uncertainty alone**. God created us for **community**, knowing that we thrive when we are surrounded by **faith-filled believers** who uplift, encourage, and strengthen us in our walk with Him.

A **strong faith community** provides:

- Encouragement—Reminding us of **God's promises** when we feel discouraged.
- **Prayer Support**—Lifting us up in prayer and standing with

us in faith.

- **Wise Counsel**—Offering **biblical wisdom** and helping us stay **grounded in truth**.

Proverbs 27:17 reminds us:

The Power of Walking Together in Faith

When we surround ourselves with **other believers**, we are better equipped to:

- **Face challenges with strength and courage.**
- **Trust in God's timing, even when waiting is difficult.**
- **Encourage one another to remain steadfast in faith.**

Who in Your Life Can Support You Spiritually?

- Do you have **a mentor or trusted friend** who points you back to God's truth?
- Are you connected to **a faith community** that can walk with you in times of uncertainty?

If not, **pray for God to bring the right people into your life**. **Faith grows stronger in community**, and together, we can walk **boldly in trust and obedience** to God's plan.

Surrendering to Trust God

Trusting God in uncertain times can be challenging. It requires us to **step beyond our comfort zones**, release our need for **control**, and fully **depend on Him**.

True trust requires:

- Courage—To take **steps of faith**, even when we don't know the outcome.
- Humility—To acknowledge that **God's ways are higher than ours** (*Isaiah 55:8-9*).
- Surrender—To let go of **our own plans** and fully embrace **His perfect will**.

When we **choose to trust** in God's **unfailing love and faithfulness**, we experience a **supernatural peace** that the world cannot give.

Philippians 4:7 assures us:

Will You Choose to Surrender?

Instead of **worrying about the unknown**, release your burdens to God and **rest in His promises. His plans are greater than your fears, and His peace will sustain you every step of the way.**

Final Reflection

As you navigate seasons of **uncertainty**, take a moment to reflect on **God's presence, faithfulness, and provision** in your life.

Ask Yourself:

1. **What are you grateful for today?**
    - Even in difficult seasons, there is always something to **thank God for**. Gratitude shifts your focus from **what's missing to what God has already done**.
2. **How can you remind yourself of God's faithfulness in uncertain moments?**
    - Consider keeping a **journal of answered prayers**, meditating on Scripture, or recalling past times when **God has guided and provided for you**.
3. **Who in your life can encourage and uplift you in your faith?**
    - Surround yourself with **faith-filled believers** who can **pray for you, speak life into you, and remind you of God's promises** when doubts arise.

Walk Forward in Faith

As you **practice gratitude, trust, and surrender**, may you find **unshakable peace and confidence** in knowing that **God is always in control and** lovingly leads you toward **His perfect plan**.

You are not alone. No matter how uncertain the path may seem, **God is guiding you every step of the way**. His presence goes before you, His strength sustains you, and His promises remain true.

How will you actively demonstrate trust in God's plan today? Will you pray, seek guidance, or take a specific step of faith? Share your plan.

Release Your Fears and Trust in God.
Welcome His Guidance into Your Life.
Consider taking a bold step in faith today. You could reach out to someone in need, establish a new prayer habit, or venture beyond your comfort zone to serve others.

God's Plan Transcends Your Uncertainties, and His Faithfulness Endures Forever.

Embracing Faith Amid Uncertainty: Choosing Trust Over Fear

Uncertainty is a natural part of life, but it doesn't have to **diminish your faith**. Instead, it can be an **opportunity to draw closer to God**. Trusting Him **when the path is unclear** is a powerful act of **worship, surrender, and faith**—one that deepens your relationship with Him.

Hold onto the promise of **Jeremiah 29:11**:

Even when life feels uncertain, **God's plans remain steady, His purpose remains sure, and His love remains unshakable**.

As you face uncertainty:

- **Hold fast to God's promises**—His **Word never fails**.
- **Trust in His goodness**—even when you don't understand, **He is working all things for your good**.
- **Take the next step in faith**—even a **small step of obedience** brings you closer to **God's perfect plan**.

What Step of Faith Will You Take Today?

- Will you surrender a fear that has been holding you back?
- Will you choose to trust Him even when you don't have all the answers?
- Will you take a step forward, believing that He is guiding you?

Release fear by surrendering specific worries to God in prayer. Replace anxious thoughts with affirmations of His promises and presence. Open your heart to God's guidance through prayer, meditation on Scripture, and seeking wisdom from trusted mentors or friends. Step forward with confidence by reflecting on past victories, affirming your strengths in Christ, and visualizing success in alignment with God's will.

Remember, God walks beside you through every challenge, offering His strength and guidance. Lean on His presence and trust in His unwavering support. As you trust Him, reflect on past instances where God's faithfulness exceeded your expectations. Anticipate His continued blessings as you remain steadfast in faith.

CHAPTER 7
CULTIVATING DAILY BRAVE MOMENTS

Bravery is not solely defined by large acts or significant accomplishments. More often, it's found in **the small, consistent acts of faith** that shape our lives and deepen our trust in God. **Each day gives you the opportunity to honor God and strengthen your faith through small acts of bravery.**

- **Cultivating daily brave moments**—choosing faith over fear in everyday situations.
- **Understanding how small acts of courage enhance spiritual strength through reflection.**
- **The encouragement to take one bold step at a time**—trusting that God meets us in each moment of bravery.

Courage in Everyday Moments

We often associate "**courage**" with dramatic, life-changing actions—**scaling mountains, confronting danger, or speaking boldly before a crowd**. While these acts of bravery are admirable, **true courage is often found in the quiet, everyday moments**—the ones that **go unnoticed by the world but are deeply significant in God's eyes**.

Bravery is choosing to trust God when:

- You step out in faith **even when the outcome is uncertain**.
- You **forgive someone** who hurt you, even when it's difficult.
- You **stand up for what is right**, even if you stand alone.
- You speak words of **encouragement and truth** in a moment of doubt.
- You take a step forward **despite fear**, knowing that God goes before you.

Joshua 1:9 reminds us:

The Power of Small, Consistent Acts of Faith

Courage is cultivated **not in a single moment but through daily choices**. Just as a muscle grows through **consistent exercise**, our faith grows stronger **each time we choose bravery over fear**.

- A **small act of obedience today** prepares you for **greater steps of faith tomorrow**.

- Trusting God each day leads to a life of strong and unwavering faith.

What specific act of bravery will you undertake today to strengthen your faith, such as forgiving someone who hurt you or speaking words of encouragement in a moment of doubt?

God calls each of us to **walk forward in courage**, trusting Him in the **big and small moments alike**. As we step out in faith, we discover that **He is with us, strengthening us, and leading us forward**.

How can you demonstrate trust in God more fully through a small act of bravery today?

The Importance of Small, Consistent Acts of Faith

Think of faith as a muscle that gets stronger with regular workouts. **Small, brave actions** taken daily **prepare us for greater faith steps** when challenges arise. Even if these moments **seem insignificant at the time**, they **build a foundation of trust and obedience**, equipping us for **bigger battles ahead**.

- *"Your servant has been keeping his father's sheep. When a lion or a bear came and carried off a sheep from the flock, I went after it, struck it, and rescued the sheep from its mouth. When it turned on me, I seized it by its hair, struck it, and killed it. Your servant has killed both the lion and the bear; this uncircumcised Philistine will be like one of them, because he has defied the armies of the living God. The Lord who rescued me from the paw of the lion and the paw of the bear will rescue me from the hand of this Philistine."* **(NIV)Small Steps of Faith Lead to Greater VictoriesWhat Small Act of Faith Can You Take Today to show kindness to someone in need?David's Early Courage and Preparation**

Before David faced

Goliath

, he had already developed

a habit of courage and faith

. As a shepherd, he protected his flock

from lions and bears

, trusting in God's strength to overcome each challenge. These small acts of bravery equipped him for the bigger challenge that lay ahead.

- *"As Jesus looked up, he saw the rich putting their gifts into the temple treasury. He also saw a poor widow put in two very small copper coins. 'Truly I tell you,' he said, 'this poor widow has put in more than all the others. All these people gave their gifts out of their wealth; but she out of her poverty put in all she had to live on.'"* **(Luke 21:1-4, NIV)Faith Grows Like a SeedlingEvery Small Act of Faith MattersWhat Small Step Will You Take Today to share your faith with someone you know?The Widow's Offering: Small Acts of Faith Matter**

In

Luke 21:1-4

, Jesus observes people

giving their offerings

at the temple. Many gave

large sums

, but it was

a poor widow's small offering

that caught His attention.

- *"Truly I tell you, whatever you did for one of the least of these brothers and sisters of mine, you did for me."* **(Matthew 25:40, NIV)Examples of Everyday Acts of Faith:Why Small Acts of Kindness MatterWhat Simple Act of Faith Can You Do Today?Daily Acts of Kindness: Faith in Action**

Faith is not just

what we believe

—it's

how we live it out daily

. Simple acts of

kindness and compassion

may seem small, but they are

powerful expressions of faith

in action.

- *"Whoever is faithful in very little is also faithful in much."* **(Luke 16:10, NIV)Examples of Overcoming Daily Temptations:Small Victories Lead to Lasting StrengthWhat Small Victory Will You Claim Today?Overcoming Daily Temptations: Small Victories That Build Strength**

Every day, we face

small but significant choices

—moments where we can

give in to temptation or choose faithfulness

. These decisions may seem minor, but they

shape our character, strengthen our faith, and prepare us for greater challenges ahead

.

- *"For God did not give us a spirit of fear and timidity, but of power, love, and self-discipline."* (**2 Timothy 1:7, NLT**).

Small Acts of Courage That Lead to Growth: Why Stepping Out in Faith MattersWhat Small Step Will You Take Today?Stepping Outside Your Comfort Zone: Growing Through Courage:

True growth happens

when we step beyond what feels safe and familiar

. While staying in our comfort zone may feel

secure

, it often limits our ability to

trust God, develop new strengths, and experience the fullness of His plans for us

.

The Power of Small, Brave Moments

Courage isn't always about **big, dramatic gestures**—sometimes, it's found in the **quiet, daily decisions** we make to **trust God and do what is right**. These **small, brave moments** may seem insignificant, but they **shape our character, strengthen our faith, and prepare us for greater challenges**.

Examples of Everyday Bravery:

- **Choosing integrity in a difficult situation.**
    - Standing firm in **truth and righteousness**, even when it's inconvenient, reflects **faith in God's justice. (Proverbs 10:9)**
- **Extending kindness to someone who has hurt you.**
    - Forgiveness and kindness, even when undeserved, are **acts of trust in God's grace and healing power. (Ephesians 4:32)**
- **Stepping outside your comfort zone to share your faith.**
    - Speaking about your faith with someone who may not understand **requires courage**, but it can **plant seeds of hope and transformation. (Romans 1:16)**

Why These Acts Matter

Each **small decision to trust God** builds:

- **Spiritual resilience**—Strengthening your faith and preparing you for future challenges.
- **A deeper relationship with God**—learning to rely on His strength in every moment.
- **A powerful testimony**—showing others what it means to **walk by faith, not by sight**.

What Brave Choice Will You Make Today?

- **Will you stand firm in integrity, even when it's hard?**
- **Will you extend grace where it's difficult?**
- **Will you dare to take a risk, even if it causes discomfort?**

Every act of **courage, kindness, and faithfulness** is seen by God. **Keep choosing bravery in the small moments, and watch how He uses them to shape you for His greater purpose!**

Journaling and Reflecting on Moments of Bravery

Reflection is a powerful tool for recognizing **God's faithfulness** and tracking **your spiritual growth**. Journaling allows you to **capture moments of courage**, no matter how small, and **see how God is working in your life**.

Writing down these experiences **helps us process our emotions**, recognize **patterns of faithfulness**, and build confidence to **continue stepping forward in courage**.

Why Journaling Matters:

- **Affirming Progress**
    - Writing about your **brave moments** helps you see **how far you've come**.
    - Small victories add up, reminding you that **courage grows with practice**.

- **Recognizing God's Presence**
  - Reflection allows you to **identify how God has guided and strengthened you**.
  - You'll begin to notice **patterns of His faithfulness** in your life. (**Psalm 77:11**)
- **Building Gratitude**
  - A journal filled with **brave moments** becomes a **testimony of God's faithfulness.**
  - Looking back on past challenges reminds you to **trust Him in the present and future.** (**1 Thessalonians 5:18**)

How to Get Started:

- **Set aside time** each day or week to reflect on **moments of courage, trust, and growth**.
- **Write honestly**—whether your step of bravery was big or small, **it matters**.
- **Look for God's hand** in your experiences and express **gratitude** for how He's working.

What Brave Moment Will You Write About Today?

Journaling isn't just about recording events—it's about **recognizing God's work, affirming your faith, and preparing for even greater steps of courage ahead. Start today, and let your story become a testimony of God's faithfulness!**

What to Journal: Capturing Your Brave Moments

Journaling is a powerful way to track your spiritual growth, recognize God's faithfulness, and gain clarity and encouragement for the future. You can include your reflections on moments of courage, answered prayers, unexpected opportunities, and lessons learned about yourself and God's character. When you document **your moments of courage**, you create a **record of God's work in your life**, reminding yourself that **He is always guiding you forward**.

What to Include in Your Journal:

1. **Your Brave Acts**
    - Write about the **moments when you stepped out in faith**, even if they seemed small.
    - These could be:
        - **Speaking up for what's right**
        - **Trying something new despite fear**
        - **Choosing to trust God instead of worrying**
2. **God's Response**

- Reflect on how **God showed up in those moments**—through:
  - **Answered prayers**
  - **Unexpected opportunities**
  - **A deep sense of peace in uncertainty**
- Look for ways He has been **faithful, present, and working in your life**.

3. **Lessons Learned:** Document what you learned about yourself, your faith, and God's character through your brave actions. Reflect on how these moments grew your trust in God, the fears you overcame, and the insights you gained into God's faithfulness.
   - Document **what you learned** about yourself, your faith, and **God's character** through your brave actions.
   - Ask yourself:
     - **How did this moment grow my trust in God?**
     - **What fears did I overcome?**
     - **What did I learn about God's faithfulness?**

Why Journaling Matters

- **Helps you track your progress and celebrate growth.**

- **Provides encouragement for future challenges.**
- **Reminds you that God is always working in your life.**

Start Today: What Brave Moment Will You Write About?

Even if it feels small, **every act of courage counts**. Take a few moments to **write, reflect, and give thanks**—and let your journal be a testimony of **God's faithfulness in your journey of bravery.**

Keeping a Journal: A Powerful Tool for Cultivating Daily Bravery

Journaling is more than just writing—it is a **powerful tool** for **building courage, strengthening faith, and deepening self-awareness**. By consistently recording your experiences, victories, and struggles, you create **a personal testimony of God's faithfulness** and **a roadmap for spiritual growth**.

Ways to Use Your Journal for Bravery:

- **Record Your Victories**
    - Note down the **small acts of courage** you exhibited throughout the day.
    - Whether it's **speaking up, choosing integrity, or trusting God in uncertainty**, acknowledging these moments:

        - **Reinforces your sense of accomplishment.**
        - **Encourages you to keep striving for greater faith and courage.**

- **Reflect on Your Challenges**
    - Journaling provides **a safe space** to process your struggles and fears.
    - Writing about your challenges **helps you identify the root of your anxieties.**
    - Once you identify the obstacles preventing you, you can devise strategies to surmount your fears and take a bold step.
- **Discover Patterns and Themes**
    - As you **review your journal entries**, you may begin to **notice recurring patterns** in:
        - Your **thoughts and emotions.**
        - How you **respond to challenges.**
        - Areas where you feel **strong or need growth.**
    - This self-reflection provides **valuable insights into your spiritual journey** and helps you identify:
        - **Strengths to celebrate.**
        - **Weaknesses to surrender to God.**

- **Growth areas where God is stretching your faith.**

Biblical Example: The Psalmist's Reflection

The **Psalmist demonstrated reflective journaling** in **Psalm 77:11-12**, recording **God's faithfulness** as a way to cultivate trust and confidence:

How to Start Your Bravery Journal Today

- **Set aside a few moments each day** to reflect and write.
- **Be honest** about both victories and struggles.
- **Look for patterns and recognize God's hand** in your journey.
- **Use Scripture** as a guide to remind yourself of **God's past faithfulness** and **His promises for the future**.

Your Story Matters

Your experiences, insights, and testimony have the power to inspire and uplift others on their courageous

journey. Consider sharing how moments of courage have shaped you, the lessons learned from stepping out in faith, and how God has strengthened you through past challenges.

Each **small act of courage** you document is **a step toward greater faith and resilience**. Over time, your journal will become **a testimony of God's presence in your life**—a powerful reminder that **He is always with you, guiding you through every challenge.**

Encouraging Readers to Take One Bold Step at a Time

Courageous living is **not about taking giant leaps every day**—it's about **being faithful in the next small step** that God places before you. Trusting Him in **small moments of bravery** builds the strength to **face bigger challenges** when they come.

Matthew 6:34 reminds us:

Instead of feeling overwhelmed by the future, focus on **what God is calling you to do today**.

Practical Ways to Take Bold Steps of Faith Daily:

1. Begin with Prayer

- **Start your day** by asking God for **guidance, wisdom, and courage**.
- Pray for **opportunities to act boldly** and for the strength

to respond **when they come**.

- Trust that **God will equip you** for whatever lies ahead.

James 1:5 promises:

What small but bold step can you take today?

- **Can you start a conversation about your faith?**
- **Can you offer kindness to someone who needs it?**
- **Can you embrace an opportunity that challenges your comfort zone?**

Every small act of courage contributes to a life characterized by faith and strength. Start today, take one step, and trust God to lead the way.

2. Identify Small Opportunities for Courage

Courage isn't always about **grand gestures**—it's often found in **the small, everyday moments** when we choose faith over fear. **Look for opportunities** to stretch your faith in your daily life. These moments may seem minor, but each one builds **spiritual resilience and trust in God**.

Here are some **simple but bold steps** you can take today:

- **Offer encouragement to a coworker or friend.**
    - A kind word can make a **huge difference** in someone's day (**Proverbs 16:24**).

- **Apologize when you've made a mistake.**
  - Owning up to our failures takes **humility and bravery** (**Colossians 3:13**).
- **Take the first step toward a long-delayed goal.**
  - Whether it's **starting a new project, pursuing a calling, or making a needed change**, small steps lead to **big transformations** (**Philippians 4:13**).

Why Small Acts of Courage Matter

- **They strengthen your faith**—teaching you to **rely on God daily**.
- **They prepare you for greater challenges**—each step builds **confidence and resilience**.
- **They reflect God's character**—demonstrating love, grace, and integrity in your actions.

Take Action Today

- **What small step of courage can you take right now?**
- **Who in your life needs encouragement or an act of kindness?**
- **What goal or challenge have you been avoiding that you can take one step toward today?**

God honors every act of bravery, no matter how small. Step forward in faith, and trust that He is leading the way!

3. Embrace Discomfort as Growth

Courage often requires stepping outside your comfort zone. Growth happens when we **trust God enough to move beyond what feels safe and familiar**. The moments that stretch us are often the ones that shape us the most.

When God calls us to **take bold steps**, it may feel uncomfortable, but **He never asks us to go alone**. He promises to **strengthen and equip us** for every challenge.

Philippians 4:13 assures us:

Why Discomfort Leads to Growth:

- **It builds spiritual strength.** Just as muscles grow stronger with resistance, **our faith strengthens when we trust God in uncertainty**.
- **It deepens our dependence on God. Stepping into discomfort teaches us to rely on His power rather than our own.**
- **It opens doors to new opportunities**—many blessings come **on the other side of fear**. Stepping out in faith allows God to **work through us in ways we never imagined**.

Take the Next Step

- **What is one area where fear is holding you back?**
- **How can you step out in faith, trusting that God will meet you there?**
- **What new opportunity or challenge is God calling you to embrace?**

Growth happens in discomfort, and courage grows through action. Step forward in faith today, knowing that Christ is your strength!

4. Celebrate Your Wins

Every brave step—no matter how small—is a victory. Choosing courage in any situation is an act of faith, and it's important to **acknowledge and thank God for the strength He provides**.

Often, we focus on **what still needs to be done**, but taking time to **celebrate progress** reminds us of **how far we've come** and strengthens our faith for what's ahead.

1 Thessalonians 5:18 encourages us:

Why Celebrating Wins Matters:

- **It reinforces your faith.** Seeing how God has helped you overcome past challenges **gives you confidence in facing new ones.**

- **It shifts your focus to gratitude**—seeing **replaces fear and doubt**, reminding you of God's goodness.
- **It builds momentum**—every small victory **fuels your motivation** to keep moving forward in faith.

How to Celebrate Your Wins:

- **Take a moment to thank God**—express gratitude for **His strength and guidance** in your journey.
- **Write down your victories**—journaling how God has helped you **creates a record of His faithfulness**.
- **Share with someone**—Encouraging others with your story **inspires them to trust God in their own challenges**.

Reflect on Your Progress

- **What small step of courage have you taken recently?**
- **How has God strengthened you through it?**
- **What can you thank Him for today?**

Courage grows when we celebrate how far God has brought us. Keep stepping forward in faith, and take time to **acknowledge every victory along the way!**

5. Keep Moving Forward

Courage is a journey, not a destination. Every step you take **strengthens your faith**, preparing you for **greater challenges and**

victories ahead. **God doesn't expect perfection**—He simply asks you to **keep trusting Him and moving forward.**

Even when the path is uncertain or progress feels slow, **God is working in you**. He is shaping your heart, building your strength, and equipping you for **the next step of faith**.

Isaiah 40:31 reminds us of the strength we find in trusting Him:

Why It's Important to Keep Moving Forward:

- **Faith grows through action**—each step of courage **deepens your trust in God**.
- **God is preparing you for more**—today's challenges are **training grounds for tomorrow's victories**.
- **He renews your strength**. You are **not alone**—God **walks with you, empowers you, and strengthens you** for the journey.

Practical Steps to Keep Going:

- **Don't dwell on past failures**—learn, **grow, and move forward** in faith.
- **Stay connected to God's promises**—His Word is **your source of strength and direction**.

- **Surround yourself with encouragement**—lean on **faith-filled friends and mentors** who will remind you to keep going.

What Step Will You Take Today?

- **Is there something God has been prompting you to do?**
- **How can you trust Him more deeply in this season?**
- **What will be your next act of faith?**

No matter where you are in your journey, keep moving forward. God is leading you, strengthening you, and preparing you for something greater.

Start Small: Cultivating a Life of Daily Courage

Don't feel **overwhelmed** by the idea of living a life of **unwavering courage. Courage is not defined by monumental leaps but by the faithful progression of one step at a time.**

Where Can You Demonstrate Greater Faith Today?

- **Choose to forgive someone who has wronged you today.**
  - Let go of bitterness and trust **God's grace to heal your heart.** (**Ephesians 4:32**)
- **Today, offer a helping hand to someone in need.**

    - Whether it's a **small act of kindness** or a moment of encouragement, your actions **reflect Christ's love. (Galatians 6:9)**

- **Today, venture beyond your comfort zone and attempt something novel.**
    - Whether it's **starting a new habit, taking on a challenge, or sharing your faith**, courage grows when you **trust God beyond what feels familiar. (Joshua 1:9)**

Every Small Step Strengthens Your Faith

Each **courageous act**, no matter how small, **builds a foundation for a life of greater faith, purpose, and impact**. Over time, these steps become **habits of bravery**, shaping a heart that **fully trusts in God's plan**.

Remember: true courage **isn't about being fearless**—it's about **facing your fears with faith** and trusting in **God's unwavering support**.

Personalize Your Journey

This chapter provides a **framework for cultivating daily bravery**, but your story **makes it unique**. Consider:

- **What moments of courage have shaped you?**
- **What lessons have you learned from stepping out in faith?**
- **How has God strengthened you through past chal-**

lenges?

Your experiences, insights, and testimony have the power to inspire and uplift others on their courageous journey.

So, what bold step will you take today? Start small. Trust big. And watch how God moves.

Encouragement to Cultivate Daily Bravery

You can choose to forgive someone who has wronged you today, offer a helping hand to someone in need, or step outside your comfort zone and try something new. These actions reflect Christ's love, build spiritual resilience, and strengthen your faith in God's guidance.

Bravery **doesn't have to be dramatic or public**. It is often found in **the quiet moments of choosing faith over fear, kindness over anger, or trust over doubt**. These **small acts of courage** may seem insignificant, but **they matter deeply to God**.

Zechariah 4:10 reminds us:

God Honors Your Small Steps of Faith

Every brave decision, regardless of its size, plays a part in shaping you into the person God has called you to be. As you take **daily steps of courage**, you will:

- **Grow in confidence**—learning to trust God more with each step.
- **Strengthen your faith**—watching how God moves through your obedience.
- **Draw closer to Him**—relying on His presence and guidance in every moment.

What Brave Step Will You Take Today?

It doesn't have to be significant; it just has to be faithful. Whether you **speak truth, extend grace, or step into an opportunity outside your comfort zone, your courage inspires others and glorifies God**.

Start today. **Step forward in faith, knowing that God is with you, leading you every step of the way.**

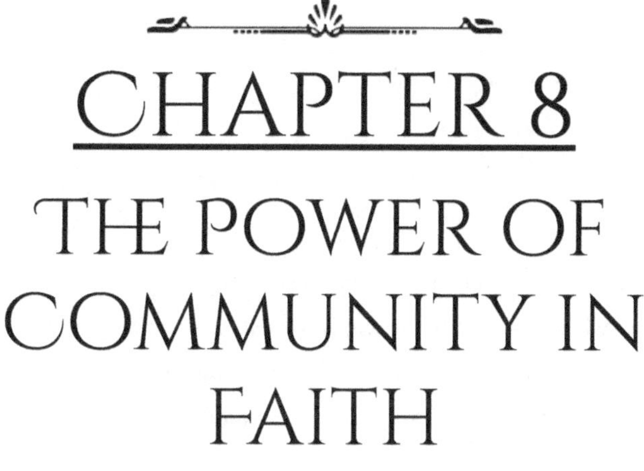

CHAPTER 8

THE POWER OF COMMUNITY IN FAITH

Faith is not meant to be lived out in isolation. From the very beginning, God designed us for **relationship, connection, and mutual encouragement**. Examples from Scripture, like the early church in Acts and the friendship between Jonathan and David, show how community inspires, sustains, and nurtures courage.

A strong community strengthens our faith, encourages us in trials, and provides guidance and accountability to help us align with the values and virtues God has called us to embody. This chapter explores:

- **How relationships inspire bravery**
- **The importance of accountability and support**
- **The transformative power of mentorship and fellowship**

Faith Flourishes in Community

Similar to how individual threads are weak but become strong when woven together into a rope, our faith becomes resilient and enduring in a supportive community.

Ecclesiastes 4:9-10 reminds us:

Faith-filled relationships provide not only encouragement but also impart wisdom and offer strength to sustain us during moments of weariness. Friendships, church fellowship, and mentorship are ways God gifts us with community to walk confidently in faith.

Examples of how community strengthens faith can include inspiring bravery, providing accountability, offering support in trials, and mentorship and fellowship.

1. **Inspiring Bravery**—Seeing others step out in faith **encourages us to do the same**.
2. **Providing Accountability**—Trusted friends help keep us **on the right path**.
3. **Offering Support in Trials**—In difficult times, community **lifts us up in prayer and love**.
4. **Mentorship and Fellowship**—Learning from others **deepens our faith and wisdom**.

Consider those who support you in faith and think about ways to enhance those relationships. Consider who encourages

you, holds you accountable, and who you inspire with your faith and courage.

- **Who encourages you when your faith feels weak?**
- **Who holds you accountable in your spiritual journey?**
- **Who do you inspire with your faith and courage?**

If you don't have a strong faith community, **pray that God will bring the right people into your life**. If you do, **be intentional about investing in those relationships**.

Community is where faith flourishes. Allow the strength of others to inspire and uplift you through God's presence among them.

Examples of how relationships can inspire and sustain courage include strengthening faith, risking personal safety to protect a friend, and choosing loyalty over personal gain.

Faith flourishes in the soil of community. God never intended for us to walk alone—He designed us to **draw strength, encouragement, and courage from one another**. When we surround ourselves with people who **believe in us, pray for us, and uplift us**, we are **better equipped to face challenges with boldness**.

Ecclesiastes 4:9-10 reminds us of the power of partnership:

In moments of **doubt, fear, or discouragement**, the **support of a faith-filled community** can be the very thing that **inspires us to keep going**.

- *"Then the Lord's anger burned against Moses and he said, 'What about your brother, Aaron the Levite? I know he can speak well. He is already on his way to meet you, and he will be glad to see you. You shall speak to him and put words in his mouth; I will help both of you speak and will teach you what to do.'"* (NIV)**Lessons from Moses and Aaron:Who Is Your Aaron?Biblical Example: Moses and Aaron**

When God called
Moses
to confront Pharaoh and lead the Israelites out of Egypt, Moses
doubted his own abilities
. He questioned whether he was the right person for the task, especially because of his
speech difficulties
.

- **A Friendship Rooted in Loyalty and Encouragement***"And Jonathan made a covenant with David because he loved him as himself. Jonathan took off the robe he was wearing and gave it to David, along with his tunic, and even his sword, his bow and his belt."* **(NIV)How Jonathan Encouraged David in His TrialsThe Life-Giving Power of Godly RelationshipsWho Is Your Jonathan?Jonathan and David: The Power of Godly Friendship**

True friendship is a gift from God, one that provides strength, encouragement, and unwavering support.

The friendship between Jonathan and David is a beautiful example of faithfulness in the Bible. Amid danger, betrayal, and uncertainty, Jonathan's support was pivotal in helping David persevere and remain faithful to God's calling.

- **A Community Rooted in Faith and Fellowship**"*They devoted themselves to the apostles' teaching and to fellowship, to the breaking of bread and to prayer. Everyone was filled with awe at the many wonders and signs performed by the apostles. All the believers were together and had everything in common. They sold property and possessions to give to anyone who had need. Every day they continued to meet together in the temple courts. They broke bread in their homes and ate together with glad and sincere hearts, praising God and enjoying the favor of all the people. And the Lord added to their number daily those who were being saved.*" **(Acts 2:42-47, NIV)Key Aspects of Their Community Life:The Power of Faith-Filled CommunityLessons for Us TodayPractical Steps to Implement the Model:The Early Church: Strength in Community**

The early believers in the book of Acts, through their devotion to teaching, fellowship, generosity, and persistent prayer, exemplify how faith thrived in their community. They

gathered together

, supported one another, and lived out their faith

in unity and love

. Their example shows us that

we are stronger when we walk together in faith

.

The Power of Community in Faith: Strength Through Connection

Human beings are inherently social creatures. We are created to **thrive in connection with others**, drawing strength from **shared experiences, mutual encouragement, and accountability**. This is especially true in our **faith journey**—when we walk alongside others, we find **greater courage, support, and perseverance.**

Proverbs 27:17 reminds us:

Why Community Matters in Our Faith Journey

- **Shared Experiences: Strength in Solidarity**
    - **Faith is not meant to be walked alone.** When we share our **struggles, triumphs, and spiritual journeys**, we **create a deep sense of connection**.
    - We discover that **we are not alone in our struggles**—others have **faced similar challenges** and emerged stronger.
    - *"Carry each other's burdens, and in this way you will fulfill the law of Christ."* **Galatians 6:2** encourages us:
- **Mutual Encouragement: A Lifeline in Difficult Times**
    - Words of **encouragement and support** from fellow

believers can **lift us up in times of doubt, fear, or discouragement**.

- Knowing that **others are praying for us and cheering us on** can give us the strength to **keep going, even when we feel weary**.
- *"And let us consider how we may spur one another on toward love and good deeds, not giving up meeting together, as some are in the habit of doing, but encouraging one another."* **Hebrews 10:24-25** reminds us:

- **Accountability and Support: Walking in Truth Together**
  - A strong faith community **challenges us to grow** by offering **accountability and support**.
  - We can **encourage one another to live out our faith**, **offer gentle correction when needed**, and **celebrate each other's victories**.
  - *"Though one may be overpowered, two can defend themselves. A cord of three strands is not quickly broken."* **Ecclesiastes 4:12** illustrates the strength of community:

Creating an Environment Where Courage Thrives

When you **surround yourself with people** who share your values and **support your spiritual growth**, you create **an environment where courage can thrive**. Community helps us:

- **Stand firm in our faith** during trials.

- **Grow spiritually through shared wisdom and accountability.**
- **Experience God's love through the support of others.**

Who Is Walking With You?

- **Do you have a community that strengthens your faith?**
- **Who in your life encourages and challenges you to trust God more deeply?**
- **How can you be a source of encouragement and support to others?**

Faith **grows best in fellowship. Surround yourself with godly relationships**, invest in them, and let your faith be strengthened **through the power of community.**

Building a Circle of Accountability and Support

Accountability and support are essential for staying on the path of **faith and courage**. A strong community **helps you remain committed to your goals, strengthens your faith, and challenges you to grow spiritually**.

Proverbs 27:17 highlights the sharpening effect of relationships:

1. What Does Accountability Look Like?

Honesty: Transparency in Faith

- True accountability **requires honesty**—being open about your **struggles, doubts, and challenges**.
- It means **inviting trusted friends** to **speak truth into your life**, even when it's difficult to hear.
- *"Therefore confess your sins to each other and pray for each other so that you may be healed."* **James 5:16** encourages us:

Encouragement: Strength in Support

- A **supportive circle** does more than just **correct**—it also **uplifts and encourages**.
- Accountability is about **growth**, and a strong faith community **celebrates your victories and encourages your progress**.
- *"Therefore encourage one another and build each other up, just as in fact you are doing."* **1 Thessalonians 5:11** reminds us:

Prayer: Inviting God into the Journey

- **Praying together** strengthens bonds and **invites God's presence and guidance** into your shared journey.
- When we lift each other up in **prayer**, we remind ourselves that we are **not alone in our struggles**.

- *"For where two or three gather in my name, there am I with them."* **Matthew 18:20** reassures us:

How to Build Your Circle of Accountability

- **Seek out trustworthy, faith-filled people** who will **support, challenge, and pray for you.**
- **Be open and vulnerable**—accountability only works when we are **willing to be honest.**
- **Encourage and uplift others** just as much as you seek support for yourself.

Who in Your Life Sharpens You?

- **Do you have people who encourage your faith and growth?**
- **Who holds you accountable in love and truth?**
- **How can you be a source of accountability and encouragement for someone else?**

Step Forward in Faith Together

We were never meant to **walk alone. Build a circle of accountability and support, and watch how God strengthens you through the power of community.**

2. How to Build a Supportive Circle

Building a strong circle of **accountability and support** requires **intentional effort and wise choices**. Surrounding yourself with people who **share your faith, encourage your growth, and hold you accountable** will strengthen your spiritual journey.

Steps to Build a Faith-Filled Support System:

1. Be Intentional: Seek Meaningful Connections

- **Look for relationships** with people who share your **faith and values**.
- Join **small groups, Bible studies, or church ministries** where you can connect with **like-minded believers**.
- *"And let us consider how we may spur one another on toward love and good deeds, not giving up meeting together, as some are in the habit of doing, but encouraging one another."* **Hebrews 10:24-25** encourages us:

2. Choose Trustworthy People: Find the Right Accountability Partners

- Look for **spiritually mature, nonjudgmental, and trustworthy** individuals.
- Accountability partners should be people who **will speak truth in love, challenge you to grow, and encourage you**

in your walk with Christ.

- *"Walk with the wise and become wise, for a companion of fools suffers harm."* **Proverbs 13:20** reminds us:

3. Be a Supporter: Give What You Seek

- Accountability requires reciprocal support and encouragement.
- Be a **source of prayer, encouragement, and wisdom** for those in your circle.
- *"Carry each other's burdens, and in this way you will fulfill the law of Christ."* **Galatians 6:2** reminds us:

Who Can You Invite Into Your Support Circle?

- **Who in your life encourages and strengthens your faith?**
- **Who do you trust to challenge and support you in your spiritual growth?**
- **How can you be a better encourager and accountability partner to someone else?**

Faith grows best in community. Be intentional about building your support circle, and watch how God uses those relationships to strengthen your walk with Him.

Cultivating Meaningful Relationships in Your Faith Community

Building strong, faith-filled relationships **doesn't happen overnight**—it is an **ongoing process** that requires **intentionality, openness, and a willingness to both give and receive support**. God designed us for **connection**, and when we invest in **authentic relationships within our faith community**, we grow **stronger in our walk with Him**.

How to Foster Meaningful Faith-Based Connections

1. Seek Out Opportunities for Connection

- **Engage in small group studies**—a great way to **grow spiritually** and **build deeper relationships**.
- **Attend church events and gatherings**—worship, fellowship, and special events help **strengthen your sense of belonging**.
- **Participate in service projects**—serving alongside others **creates lasting bonds** and **reflects Christ's love** in action.

2. Be Intentional About Building Relationships

- **Go beyond surface-level conversations**—ask meaningful questions and **show genuine interest in others' lives**.
- **Be open about your struggles and triumphs**—authenticity fosters trust and **deepens connections**.
- **Make time for relationships**—invest in friendships through **coffee meetups, phone calls, or shared activities**.

3. Offer Support to Others

- **Be a source of encouragement**—listen, pray, and offer words of hope.
- **Look for ways to serve others**—whether through practical help, emotional support, or simply being present.
- **Be the kind of friend you seek**—relationships are strongest when **both giving and receiving are valued**.

Start Building Your Faith Community Today

- Who in your church or small group can you connect with on

a deeper level?

- How can you be more intentional about fostering meaningful relationships?
- What small step can you take today to support or encourage someone in your faith circle?

When we cultivate strong, faith-centered relationships, we create an environment where love, encouragement, and spiritual growth thrive. Invest in your faith community, and watch how God strengthens your journey through the people around you.

The Role of Mentorship and Fellowship in Strengthening Faith

Mentorship and fellowship are powerful tools that **nurture spiritual growth, provide wisdom, and foster a deep sense of belonging** in the body of Christ. While mentors offer **guidance and insight**, fellowship provides **mutual encouragement and accountability**. Both play a crucial role in **helping us walk boldly in faith**.

1. The Impact of Mentorship

A **mentor** is someone who has walked the path of faith **longer** and can offer **wisdom, encouragement, and support**. Seeking guidance from **a trusted spiritual mentor** can help you:

- **Gain valuable insights** into God's plan for your life.
- **Receive encouragement** during difficult seasons.
- **Navigate the complexities of life** with biblical wisdom.
- **Be equipped for leadership and service** in God's king-

dom.

Proverbs 19:20 reminds us:

- **Moses and Joshua, Paul and Timothy are Biblical Examples of Mentorship**
  - **Moses mentored Joshua**, preparing him to **lead the Israelites into the Promised Land**.
  - Before stepping into leadership, Joshua **learned from Moses' example**, witnessing God's power and guidance.
  - *"Be strong and courageous, for you must go with this people into the land that the Lord swore to their ancestors to give them, and you must divide it among them as their inheritance."* **Deuteronomy 31:7-8** records Moses' encouragement to Joshua:
  - **Paul served as a spiritual father to Timothy**, equipping him to **lead the early church**.
  - Paul encouraged Timothy to **remain strong in faith** and to pass on the wisdom he received.
  - *"You then, my son, be strong in the grace that is in Christ Jesus. And the things you have heard me say in the presence of many witnesses entrust to reliable people who will also be qualified to teach others."* **2 Timothy 2:1-2** highlights this:

- **Finding a Mentor**
    - **Pray** for God to lead you to **a mentor who can guide you spiritually**.
    - Look for individuals **whose lives reflect a deep relationship with Christ**.
    - Seek someone **who is willing to invest in your growth** and walk alongside you in faith.
    - **Be teachable**—mentorship is most effective when you're open to learning and receiving correction.

Who Can Be a Mentor in Your Life?

- Who do you admire for their faith and wisdom?
- Who has walked a similar path and can offer guidance?
- How can you seek their wisdom and build a mentorship relationship?

Mentorship is a gift that strengthens our faith and equips us to fulfill God's purpose. Seek wise counsel, invest in meaningful relationships, and let God use others to guide you on your journey of faith.

2. The Power of Fellowship

Fellowship provides unity, encouragement, and a shared purpose in Christ. When believers come together, they **strengthen one another**, build **lasting relationships**, and reflect **God's love in action**.

In a world that often promotes **independence and self-reliance**, God calls us to **walk together in faith**, lifting one another up and growing in spiritual maturity **through connection with other believers**.

Hebrews 10:24-25 reminds us:

Ways to Cultivate Fellowship in Your Faith Journey

- **Worship Together**
    - Joining others in worship **reminds us that we are part of something bigger than ourselves**.
    - Corporate worship **uplifts the spirit, strengthens our faith, and connects us to God in unity**.
    - *"Come, let us bow down in worship, let us kneel before the Lord our Maker."* **Psalm 95:6** calls us to worship together:
- **Serve Together**
    - Working alongside others in **ministry, outreach, or service projects** deepens relationships and demonstrates **God's love in action**.
    - Serving together **teaches humility, teamwork, and compassion**, reflecting Christ's heart for the world.

- *"Each of you should use whatever gift you have received to serve others, as faithful stewards of God's grace in its various forms."* **1 Peter 4:10** reminds us:

- **Why Fellowship MattersHow Can You Engage in Fellowship Today?Bear One Another's Burdens**
    - *"Carry each other's burdens, and in this way you will fulfill the law of Christ."* **Galatians 6:2** urges us:
    - True fellowship means **supporting one another through trials, challenges, and hardships**.
    - When we **share in each other's struggles**, we reflect **God's compassion and faithfulness**.
    - **It provides encouragement**—helping us remain strong in our faith during difficult seasons.
    - **It fosters accountability**—encouraging us to stay true to God's Word and purpose.
    - **It builds a sense of belonging**—reminding us that **we are never alone in our faith journey**.
    - Can you join a Bible study or prayer group?
    - Who in your community needs encouragement or support?
    - How can you use your gifts to serve others in faith?

The Transformative Power of Community in Faith

The power of **community in faith** cannot be overstated. God never intended for us to **walk alone**—He designed us to **thrive in relationships**, drawing strength from one another as we grow in Him.

When we **cultivate meaningful relationships** within our faith community, we experience the **transformative power of love, support, and encouragement**. Through these relationships, we can:

- **Learn from one another**—gaining wisdom, insight, and spiritual growth.
- **Grow together**—Strengthening our faith as we walk alongside fellow believers.
- **Face life's challenges with renewed strength and confidence**—knowing we have **God's presence and the support of a faith-filled community**.

Romans 12:10 reminds us:

Why Community Matters in Our Faith Journey

- **Encouragement in Difficult Times**—Support from fellow believers helps us remain steadfast in faith.
- **Accountability and Growth**— A strong faith community **challenges us to grow spiritually**.
- **The Joy of Fellowship**—Walking together in faith **brings unity, purpose, and deeper connection with God**.

How Will You Invest in Your Faith Community Today?

- **Will you reach out to someone who needs encouragement?**
- **Will you join a small group, Bible study, or ministry team?**
- **Will you embrace the power of fellowship and walk boldly in faith alongside others?**

God designed us for connection. Lean into community, offer support, and allow your faith to be strengthened through the love and encouragement of those around you.

Practical Steps to Cultivate Community

Building a strong faith community requires **intentionality and prayer**. Relationships that **uplift, encourage, and strengthen our faith** don't always happen by chance—they develop when we **seek God's guidance and take steps to connect with others**.

1. Pray for Divine Connections

Before seeking relationships, **seek God first**. Ask Him to **bring the right people into your life**—those who will **support your faith journey, challenge you to grow, and walk alongside you in love and truth**.

Proverbs 16:9 reminds us:

How to Pray for the Right Relationships:

- **Ask God to lead you to people who will strengthen your faith.**
- **Pray for wisdom** in choosing friendships that **align with His will**.
- **Seek opportunities to be a blessing to others**, not just to receive support.

Trust that God will establish the relationships you need at the right time. Your role is to step out in faith and be open to His guidance.

2. Join a Small Group or Ministry

Be proactive in seeking community. Meaningful relationships develop when you take intentional steps to connect with others who share your faith.

Many churches offer **small groups, Bible studies, or service opportunities** where you can:

- **Build relationships** with like-minded believers.
- **Grow spiritually** through shared learning and discussion.
- **Serve others** while deepening your sense of purpose.

Acts 2:46-47 gives us an example of the early church's commitment to fellowship:

How to Get Involved:

- **Visit your church's small groups or ministry directory** and find one that interests you.
- **Attend a Bible study or prayer group** to connect with others in faith.
- **Join a service or outreach ministry** to build relationships while making an impact.

By taking the step to **actively engage in community**, you allow God to **use others to encourage and strengthen your faith**—and He may also use **you** to be a blessing to someone else!

3. Be Vulnerable

Authenticity builds deeper connections. True community is not just about **being present**—it's about **being real**. When we share our **challenges, victories, doubts, and joys**, we invite others to **walk alongside us** in our faith journey.

Some individuals struggle in isolation due to the fear of judgment or being misunderstood by others. However, God calls us to **live in truth and love**, supporting one another through **honest, meaningful relationships**.

James 5:16 encourages us:

Why Vulnerability Matters in Faith Community:

- **It fosters trust**—when you open up, others feel safe to do the same.
- **It deepens relationships**—honest conversations create **genuine connections**.
- **It strengthens faith**—sharing your struggles **reminds you that you're not alone** and allows others to **encourage and uplift you in prayer**.

Practical Steps to Practice Vulnerability in Community:

- **Share your story**—open up about how God has worked in your life.
- **Ask for prayer**—let others support you spiritually.
- **Be honest about struggles and victories**—encourage others by sharing both your challenges and the ways you've seen God's faithfulness.

Being vulnerable opens the door for God to work through others in our lives, fostering spiritual growth and deeper connections. True faith community grows when we choose authenticity over isolation.

4. Invest in Relationships

Strong relationships require effort and intentionality. Building community is a deliberate process that involves investing time, offering encouragement, and praying for others.

Romans 12:10 reminds us:

Steps to Strengthen Relationships:

1. Be Present

- Make time for **regular fellowship** with your faith community.
- Participate in church events and gatherings to foster community connections.

2. Encourage Others

- Provide encouragement, kindness, and support to those in your circle.
- *"Therefore encourage one another and build each other up, just as in fact you are doing."*"**1 Thessalonians 5:11** says:

3. Pray for Your Community

- Prayer is one of the most **powerful ways to invest in relationships**.
- Lift up others in **prayer for their needs, struggles, and**

spiritual growth.

- **Job 42:10** teaches that Job's **own restoration came when he prayed for his friends.**

Commit to Investing in Others

- **Who in your faith community needs encouragement?**
- **How can you intentionally spend time strengthening your relationships?**
- **Who can you pray for today?**

When we invest in relationships with love, time, and prayer, we strengthen the body of Christ and experience the true power of faith-filled community.

5. Mentor and Be Mentored

Spiritual growth thrives in the cycle of learning and teaching. Seeking guidance from a **mentor** while also investing in someone **earlier in their faith journey** creates a **powerful dynamic of encouragement, accountability, and discipleship**.

Proverbs 9:9 highlights the importance of this cycle:

The Significance of Mentorship in Faith:

- **A mentor provides wisdom and direction.**

- They offer **spiritual guidance, encouragement, and accountability**.
- They help navigate **challenges, doubts, and decisions** with biblical wisdom.

- **Being a mentor strengthens your faith.**
  - Teaching others **deepens your own understanding** of God's Word.
  - Investing in someone else **cultivates patience, love, and humility**.

Biblical Examples of Mentorship

- **Moses and Joshua**—Moses trained Joshua to **lead the Israelites into the Promised Land (Deuteronomy 31:7-8)**.
- **Paul and Timothy**—Paul discipled Timothy, equipping him to **lead and teach in the early church** (**2 Timothy 2:1-2**).
- **Jesus and His Disciples—Jesus invested in His disciples, teaching them important lessons and skills to carry out His mission after He ascended.**

Tips for Finding a Mentor and Becoming One Yourself: 1. Seek a Mentor for Yourself by... 2. Invest in Someone Else by...

1. Seek a Mentor for Yourself

- Pray for **God to lead you to someone spiritually mature**.
- Look for individuals **who reflect a deep relationship with Christ**.
- Be **open to learning, accountability, and correction**.

2. Invest in Someone Else

- Ask God to show you **someone who needs encouragement**.
- Offer **guidance, support, and biblical wisdom** to a newer believer.
- Lead by example—**live a life that points others to Christ**.

Who Can You Learn From and Who Can You Invest In?

- Who in your life could mentor you in faith?
- Who could benefit from your encouragement and guidance?
- How can you commit to both learning and leading in your faith community?

The Reciprocal Nature of Mentorship: Mentorship is a two-way blessing where both parties share wisdom, experiences, and insights. It involves not only receiving guidance but also giving back by mentoring others, creating a cycle of growth and encouragement.

Mentorship is a two-way blessing. It is not just about receiving wisdom but also about **sharing what you have learned with others**. The beauty of mentorship is that **both giving and receiving enrich your faith journey**, deepening your understanding of God and strengthening your spiritual walk.

A Cycle of Growth and Encouragement

- **Be willing to learn from those ahead of you** – Seek guidance from those who have walked the path of faith longer and can offer wisdom, encouragement, and biblical insight.
- **Pour into those behind you** – Invest in someone who is earlier in their faith journey, sharing your experiences and helping them navigate their own walk with Christ.
- **Grow together** – Mentorship is not just about knowledge but about walking in faith **together**, strengthening one another along the way.

2 Timothy 2:2 captures this principle:

How can you actively engage in passing on your faith to the next generation? What specific actions can you take to mentor younger individuals or share your faith journey with them?

Faith and wisdom are meant to be shared. When we **receive encouragement and guidance**, we become **better equipped** to pour into others. This creates **a lasting legacy of faith**, ensuring that **God's truth continues to impact lives beyond our own**.

Who Can You Learn From and Who Can You Mentor?

- **Who has God placed in your life as a mentor?**
- **Who can you encourage, support, and guide in their faith?**
- **How can you actively engage in both giving and receiving mentorship?**

When we embrace both roles—learner and teacher—we experience the fullness of spiritual growth. Engage in mentorship today, and watch how God uses these relationships to shape your faith and the lives of those around you.

Take practical steps to embrace community: Reach out to join a small group or Bible study. Volunteer for church activities to connect with others. Initiate conversations with fellow believers to build supportive relationships.

God created us to live in relationships with others. He designed us to **thrive in connection, support and strengthen one another, and walk in faith together.**

Community is **not just a convenience—it is a divine gift.** It is a source of **strength when we are weak, encouragement when we doubt, and inspiration when we feel weary.** Through meaningful relationships, we experience **God's love, wisdom, and presence in tangible ways.**

God Designed Us for Community: Through community, we experience God's love, support, and presence tangibly. It is in connecting with others that we grow spiritually, find strength, and fulfill God's purposes together.

Hebrews 10:24-25 reminds us:

- **We are not meant to do life alone.**
- **Faith flourishes in connection**—when we gather, worship, pray, and encourage one another.
- **Together, we are stronger, braver, and more capable of fulfilling God's purposes.**

Remember, you are not alone on this journey. Seek support from your church community, a close friend, or a

spiritual mentor. Allow others to walk alongside you and uplift you in your faith walk.

God has placed **people in your life** to support you, just as He has **called you to support others**. The body of Christ is built on **love, unity, and shared faith**, and through it, we:

- Find strength in difficult times.
- Grow spiritually through accountability and wisdom.
- Experience the joy of belonging and encouragement.

Take the Next Step: Invite a friend to attend a church event with you. Join a community service project to connect with like-minded individuals. Schedule regular prayer meetings with fellow believers to deepen your bonds of faith.

- **Take steps today to build a community of faith and courage. What specific actions will you take?**
- **Who can you reach out to for encouragement, support, or mentorship?**
- **How can you invest in others, sharing the love and wisdom God has given you?**

Reach out, build relationships, and invest in fellowship. Witness how God strengthens, sustains, and inspires you through these connections in your walk of faith. Remember, you were never meant to walk alone. Embrace the power of community today for strength and support on your journey.

CHAPTER 9

LEAVING A LEGACY OF COURAGEOUS FAITH

Our lives are about more than the moments we experience; they are also about the legacy we leave behind. A legacy of **courageous faith** inspires others to **trust God, live boldly, and obey His calling**.

Our words, actions, and how we handle life's challenges can influence the faith of future generations. This chapter explores:

- **How to inspire others through your testimony.**
- **How to live a life of trust in God.**
- **How to leave a lasting impact that reflects His glory.**

The Power of a Faithful Legacy

Although our lives may seem short, they have the potential to create a lasting impact on the world. Whether we realize it or not, **we are all architects of the future**, shaping it through:

- The choices we make today have the power to shape the future for generations to come.
- The actions we take today, such as showing kindness to a struggling neighbor, can have a lasting impact on the future and influence generations ahead.
- The stories we share about our experiences and beliefs play a crucial role in shaping the values and beliefs of future generations.

The faith we demonstrate today, like staying hopeful during challenging times, becomes an example for those who come after us. **Psalm 145:4** reminds us:

What Does It Mean to Leave a Legacy of Courageous Faith?

1. **Living Boldly for Christ**
    - A life of faith and obedience carries more weight than mere words.
    - *"Let your light shine before others, that they may see your good deeds and glorify your Father in heaven."* **Matthew**

5:16 encourages us:

2. **Sharing Your Testimony**

   - Your experience of relying on God during a financial crisis can motivate and uplift others.
   - *"They triumphed over him by the blood of the Lamb and by the word of their testimony."* **Revelation 12:11** declares:

3. **Investing in Others**

   - **Mentorship, discipleship, and encouragement** ensure that faith continues beyond your own lifetime.
   - *"And the things you have heard me say in the presence of many witnesses entrust to reliable people who will also be qualified to teach others."* **2 Timothy 2:2** emphasizes passing on faith:

4. **Leaving a Mark Through Love and Service**

   - Faith without action is **incomplete**. **Acts of love, service, and kindness build a legacy of faith**.
   - *"The only thing that counts is faith expressing itself through love."* **Galatians 5:6** reminds us:

What Will Your Faith Legacy Be?

- How are you actively living out your trust in God today?

- Who in your life can your story inspire and encourage?
- What specific steps can you actively pursue to ensure that your faith continues to impact others even after you're no longer present?

Your **faith, courage, and obedience** can **ignite hope and strength in future generations. Live boldly, trust fully, and leave a legacy that glorifies God.**

Inspiring Others Through Your Testimony

Your story is one of the most powerful tools you have to inspire others. Testimonies of **God's faithfulness, especially in the face of challenges,** can **ignite courage and faith** in those who hear them.

Revelation 12:11 reminds us:

Sharing your testimony **is not just about recounting past events—it is about demonstrating the power of God at work in your life.** Your journey of faith, such as overcoming a serious illness, can encourage, uplift, and strengthen those who are walking through their own struggles.

1. Be Authentic

People connect with vulnerability and honesty. Share not just the **victories and breakthroughs**, but also the **struggles, fears, and doubts** you faced along the way. Authenticity allows others to see that **faith is not about perfection but about trusting God in every circumstance.**

Paul's Transformation

The Apostle Paul was once a **persecutor of Christians,** actively working against the gospel. However, after encountering Jesus, he became one of the **greatest messengers of the faith**. He did not hide his past; instead, he used his testimony to **showcase God's power and grace.**

Acts 9 recounts Paul's dramatic conversion, while **Philippians 3:7-11** captures his new perspective:

Paul's testimony inspired countless believers to trust in the **transforming power of God's grace**—proving that **no one is beyond redemption.**

Tips for Sharing Your Story

- **Be real**—share both the struggles and the triumphs.
- **Point to Christ**—Your story should always highlight **God's faithfulness**.
- **Encourage others**— Remind your listeners that **what God has done for you, He can do for them too**.

Who Needs to Hear Your Testimony?

- **Is there someone struggling with a challenge you've overcome?**
- **How can your story encourage and strengthen their faith?**
- **Are you willing to be open and honest about what God has done in your life?**

Your story of overcoming addiction has the potential to motivate and encourage others. Be bold in sharing it, and let God use your story to bring hope and faith to those around you.

2. Highlight God's Faithfulness

Your testimony **is not just about what you've overcome**—it's about **what God has done** in your life. Always emphasize His faithfulness, provision, and love, showing how He has been present in both your challenges and triumphs.

Lamentations 3:22-23 reminds us:

As you share your story, remember to highlight God's faithfulness by addressing the following questions:

- **How did God provide for you in difficult times?**
- **How did He strengthen you when you felt weak?**
- **What lessons did He teach you through your experiences?**

Example: The Faithfulness of Joseph

Joseph's life was filled with **betrayal, hardship, and injustice**—sold into slavery by his own brothers, wrongfully imprisoned, and forgotten. Yet, despite the challenges, **he remained faithful to God**. In return, God **elevated him to a position of influence**, using him to **save many lives**.

Joseph recognized God's hand at work and declared in **Genesis 50:20**:

Joseph's story wasn't just about his suffering—it was about how God used his trials for a greater purpose.

Showcasing God's Faithfulness in Your Story

1. **Keep the focus on God, not just your struggles.**
   - Instead of only describing the hardship, emphasize **how God sustained you through it.**
2. **Share particular instances of how God has provided for you in times of need.**
   - Did He answer a prayer? Give you peace in uncertainty? Open unexpected doors?
3. **Show how His faithfulness changed you.**
   - Did you grow stronger in your faith? Learn to trust Him

more?

Reflect on Your Story

- **Where have you seen God's faithfulness in your life?**
- **How has His provision or love shaped your journey?**
- **Who needs to hear your testimony to be reminded of God's goodness?**

Your story reflects God's faithfulness. **Share it boldly, knowing that it can inspire others to trust Him in their own journey.**

3. Purposeful Story Sharing

Your testimony is a gift, meant to encourage and inspire others in their faith journey. Be **Your testimony has the power to uplift, challenge, and strengthen others.** Being intentional about sharing your faith journey can **lead someone closer to Christ** and inspire them to trust in God's faithfulness.

Whether in **personal conversations, mentoring relationships, or public platforms**, your story can make a lasting impact.

Examples of How Sharing Your Story Can Inspire Others

1. Encouraging Someone Facing a Similar Struggle

Imagine a young woman struggling with self-worth and doubt. She hears a testimony from someone who once felt the same but found

confidence and identity in Christ. That testimony reminds her that **God's love is unchanging and unconditional.**

Biblical Example:

- **The Woman at the Well (John 4:39-42)** – After Jesus revealed the truth of her life, she **ran to her community** and shared her story. Because of her **testimony**, many believed in Christ.

2. Strengthening a New Believer

A new Christian may feel overwhelmed and uncertain about their faith journey. Hearing a testimony about **someone who once struggled with doubt but grew in faith** can reassure them that growth takes time and that God is patient and faithful.

Biblical Example:

- **Paul's Transformation (Acts 9, Philippians 3:7-11)** – Paul openly shared how he went from persecuting Christians to becoming one of the greatest apostles. His testimony strengthened new believers and demonstrated **God's grace and power to transform lives.**

3. Challenging Someone to Step Out in Faith

Perhaps someone is hesitant to obey God's calling on their life. When they hear a testimony of **how someone took a leap of faith, trusted God, and saw His provision**, they may feel encouraged to do the same.

Biblical Example:

- **Peter Walking on Water (Matthew 14:28-31)**—Peter's

bold step of faith serves as an example for all believers that when we trust in Christ, He will sustain us, even when circumstances seem impossible. **Why Sharing Your Testimony Matters**

Romans 10:14 reminds us of the importance of speaking out:

When you share your testimony, you:

- **Motivate someone to embark on their next journey of faith.**
- **Show that they are not alone in their struggles.**
- **Demonstrate the power of God's grace and transformation.**

Ways to Share Your Testimony Intentionally

1. Through Personal Conversations

- Share your faith journey with **friends, family, or colleagues** in a natural and authentic way.
- Be open to **listening as much as speaking**, allowing your testimony to foster meaningful dialogue.

Mentoring and Discipling Others

- If you are mentoring someone in faith, share **how God has worked in your life** to encourage them in their walk.
- Your personal experiences can serve as **examples of God's faithfulness and guidance.**

3. On Public Platforms

- Consider sharing your testimony through **speaking engagements, writing, podcasts, or social media.**
- Your story could **reach and impact people you may never meet in person.**

Follow the Holy Spirit's lead.

Not every moment is the right time to share every part of your story. **Pray for discernment** and let the Holy Spirit guide you in:

- **Who needs to hear your testimony?**
- **How much of your story to share.**
- **When and where to speak.**

Who Needs to Hear Your Story?

- Is there someone in your life struggling with something you've overcome?

- Where can you share your testimony to encourage others?
- How can you leverage your personal experiences to bring hope and faith into the lives of those around you?

Your story has power—don't keep it to yourself. Share with intention, knowing that God can use your testimony to change lives and lead others to a deeper trust in Him.

Our Lives as Testimonies of Faith

Our lives become testimonies—living testaments to the **power of faith and God's transformative grace**. Every experience, trial, and triumph is an opportunity to **reflect His goodness and inspire others to trust in Him**.

2 Corinthians 3:3 reminds us:

We don't just share testimonies—we **become** them through the way we live.

- **Sharing Your Story**
- *"Faith by itself, if it is not accompanied by action, is dead."* **(NIV)How to Model Courageous Faith:Your Life Is a WitnessModeling Courageous Living**

Actions speak louder than words.
The way you live your life—your
integrity, compassion, and service
—demonstrates the

transformative power of faith in action

•

Living a Life That Reflects Trust in God's Purpose

Legacy is not just about what we say; it's about how we live. A life that reflects **trust in God inspires others to seek Him and trust His purposes for their lives.** True faith is not merely spoken—it is lived out daily through **obedience, surrender, and unwavering confidence in God's plans.**

1. Obedience as a Witness

Living in obedience to God is one of the most powerful ways to demonstrate a faith that is **active and real.** Our actions serve as **a testimony of God's transforming power**, showing others what it means to truly follow Christ.

James 2:18 highlights the importance of faith in action:

Why Obedience Matters:

- **It reflects a genuine faith**—obedience to God's Word shows that we trust Him fully.
- **It sets an example for others**—our lives become a witness to the power of God's grace and direction.
- **It deepens our relationship with God**—when we obey, we align our lives with **His perfect plan and purpose.**

Biblical Example: Noah's Obedience

- Noah obeyed God **even when it didn't make sense**—he built an ark in preparation for a flood when there was no sign of rain.
- His faith and obedience **saved his family and preserved God's promise**.
- *"Noah did everything just as God commanded him."* **Genesis 6:22** testifies to his trust in God:

How to Live a Life of Obedience and Trust in God's Purpose

- **Seek God's will daily**—through prayer and Scripture, allow God to direct your steps.
- **Act on faith, not fear**—trust that even when obedience is difficult, God's plans are good.
- **Be a witness through your actions**—let your life inspire others to seek God.

Reflection: Are You Living in Obedience?

- **What is one area where God is calling you to greater obedience?**

- **How can your actions reflect a faith that is real and transformative?**
- **Who in your life might be encouraged by your trust in God's purpose?**

When we live with obedience and trust in God's purpose, we leave a legacy that speaks long after we are gone. Let your faith be visible—not just in words, but in the way you live every day.

2. Resilience in Trials

How you respond to challenges speaks volumes about your faith. Trials are inevitable, but when we face them **with grace, courage, and unwavering trust in God**, our lives become a powerful testimony of **His sustaining power**.

Psalm 46:1 declares:

Resilience in the face of trials is not about ignoring pain or pretending difficulties don't exist. Instead, it is about **leaning on God's strength** and allowing Him to carry us through.

Why Resilience Matters in Faith

- **It demonstrates unwavering trust in God's sovereignty.**
- **It inspires and strengthens others** who are facing their own struggles.
- **It deepens your spiritual growth** by strengthening your dependence on God.

Biblical Example: Job's Faithfulness

- Job endured **unimaginable suffering—losing his wealth, health, and family**—yet he remained faithful to God.
- Despite his pain, he declared, **"The Lord gave and the Lord has taken away; may the name of the Lord be praised." (Job 1:21, NIV)**
- His story reminds us that **God restores and rewards faithfulness in trials.**

How to Cultivate Resilience in Your Faith Journey

- **Turn to God in prayer** – Seek His comfort and strength in difficult moments.
- **Stand on His promises** – Meditate on Scriptures that remind you of His faithfulness.
- **Find strength in community** – Surround yourself with believers who will uplift and encourage you.

Reflection: How Do You Respond to Challenges?

- **Do you turn to God first when facing difficulties?**
- **How can your response to trials encourage others to trust in God?**

- **What scriptures can you lean on in moments of hardship?**

Your resilience in trials is a testimony of God's sustaining power. By facing difficulties with faith and courage, you leave a legacy of trust in God's unshakable strength.

3. Reflecting Christ's Love

Living a life of love, generosity, and kindness mirrors Christ's character and draws others to Him. Our actions—how we treat others, how we serve, and how we show compassion—speak louder than words.

Jesus said in Matthew 5:16:

The Significance of Reflecting Christ's Love

- **It points people to God.** When we love unconditionally, we reflect **His nature** to the world.
- **It breaks down barriers.** Acts of kindness and grace **open doors for meaningful relationships and conversations about faith**.
- **It strengthens your witness.** People are more likely to listen to someone whose **life reflects the love of Christ**.

Biblical Example: The Good Samaritan

- In **Luke 10:25-37**, Jesus tells the parable of the Good Samaritan, who:
    - **Showed compassion** to a stranger.
    - **Demonstrated generosity** by caring for his needs.
    - **Acted selflessly**, expecting nothing in return.
- His actions reflected **Christ's command to love our neighbors as ourselves (Mark 12:31)**.

How to Reflect Christ's Love Daily

- **Be intentional about kindness** – A smile, a kind word, or a simple act of service can brighten someone's day.
- **Give generously** – Whether through time, resources, or encouragement, **look for ways to serve others selflessly**.
- **Forgive readily** – Extend grace and **let go of bitterness**, just as Christ forgave us (**Colossians 3:13**).

Reflection: Are You a Reflection of Christ's Love?

- How do your actions demonstrate God's love to others?
- Who in your life needs encouragement, kindness, or generosity today?
- What intentional actions can you take to more effectively reflect Christ's love in your daily interactions?

When we live with love, generosity, and kindness, we become a light in the darkness, drawing others closer to God. Let your life be a testimony that leads others to Christ through the power of His love.

Living a Life of Significance Through God's Purpose

A **life lived in accordance with God's purpose** is not about **achieving personal greatness or accumulating wealth**. Instead, it is about **living a life of significance**—one that **impacts others, glorifies God, and leaves a lasting difference in the world**.

Ephesians 2:10 reminds us:

True significance comes from **aligning our lives with God's plan** and using our gifts to serve others.

- **How to Identify Your God-Given Gifts:** *"We have different gifts, according to the grace given to each of us."* **Discovering Your God-Given Gifts and Talents**

God has given each of us

unique gifts, talents, and passions

to be used for His glory. Recognizing and using these abilities allows us to

fulfill our purpose

and

serve others effectively

.

- **How to Pursue Your Calling:** *"For I know the plans I have for you," declares the Lord, "plans to prosper you and not to* *harm you, plans to give you hope and a future."* **Embracing Your Calling**

Once you recognize your gifts, the next step is to
embrace your calling with passion and dedication
. No matter the obstacles, trusting God's plan and walking in obedience leads to
a fulfilling and purpose-driven life
.

- *"For even the Son of Man did not come to be served, but to serve, and to give His life as a ransom for many."* **Ways to Serve Others and Make a Difference:Reflection: How Are You Living a Life of Purpose?Living a Life of Service**

A
life of true significance
is a life of
service
. Jesus Himself set the ultimate example, stating in
Mark 10:45
:

Practical Ways to Make a Lasting Impact on Future Generations

Leaving a legacy of courageous faith requires **intentional actions** that **inspire, nurture, and equip others** to trust in God. **Your faith's impact today can ripple through generations**, shaping the lives of those who come after you.

1. **Building Meaningful Relationships**

One of the most effective ways to leave a legacy is by **building meaningful relationships** that cultivate faith and spiritual growth.

- **Mentor Others**
  - **Pour into the lives of those around you** by sharing your **wisdom, experiences, and encouragement**.
  - Like **Paul with Timothy**, mentoring can shape someone's spiritual journey and **equip them to grow in faith**.
  - *"I am reminded of your sincere faith, which first lived in your grandmother Lois and in your mother Eunice and, I am persuaded, now lives in you also."* **2 Timothy 1:5-6** highlights Paul's encouragement to Timothy:
- **Reflection: How Can You Invest in Others?Model Faith for Your Family**
  - **Teach your children, grandchildren, or loved ones** to trust God by **living out your faith consistently**.
  - Be a **living example of prayer, integrity, and godly wisdom**.
  - *"Start children off on the way they should go, and even when they are old they will not turn from it."* **Proverbs 22:6** reminds us:
  - **Who in your life can benefit from your guidance and encouragement?**
  - **Are you setting an example of faith for your family**

and loved ones?

- **What steps can you take today to intentionally pour into others?**

Preserve and Share Your Faith Journey

One of the most powerful ways to leave a **lasting impact** is to **preserve and share your faith journey**. By documenting **God's faithfulness**, you provide **future generations with inspiration, encouragement, and a tangible record of His work in your life.**

- **Write Your Testimony**
  - **Share how God has worked in your life**—the trials you've faced, the prayers He has answered, and the ways He has shaped your faith.
  - **Your story can inspire future generations and help them** understand **how faith in God brings hope, resilience, and victory**.
  - *"We will not hide them from their descendants; we will tell the next generation the praiseworthy deeds of the Lord, His power, and the wonders He has done."***Psalm 78:4** reminds us:
- **Reflection: How Will You Preserve Your Faith Legacy?The Power of Documenting Your Faith Journey-Why Documenting Your Faith Journey Matters** *"Let this be written for a future generation, that a people not yet created may praise the Lord."* **(NIV)1. Remembering God's Goodness2. Passing Down Faith to Future Generations3. Encouraging Others in Their Walk with God-**

Ways to Document Your Faith Legacy*"Write the vision and make it plain on tablets, that he may run who reads it."***Create a Family Legacy Book**

- **Record significant milestones, answered prayers, and key Scriptures** that have guided your journey.
- Include **letters of encouragement** for your children, grandchildren, or future generations.
- *"In the future, when your children ask you, 'What do these stones mean?' tell them that the flow of the Jordan was cut off before the ark of the covenant of the Lord."***Joshua 4:6-7** illustrates the importance of remembrance:
- What are some moments in your faith journey that could inspire others?
- What steps can you take today to start documenting your testimony and experiences of God's faithfulness?
- Who in your family or community would benefit from reading about God's work in your life?

3. Serve Your Community

A **legacy of faith** is not just about what we believe—it's about how we **live out** that belief. **Serving others** is one of the most powerful ways to reflect **God's love** and leave a lasting impact on the world. When we actively **serve our communities**, we demonstrate what it means to **live by faith, love selflessly, and be Christ's hands and feet.**

- **Act on Your Faith**

- **Faith in action inspires others.** Engaging in **acts of service**—whether through **volunteering, supporting charitable causes, or simply helping a neighbor**—brings God's love into tangible reality.
- *"Faith by itself, if it is not accompanied by action, is dea d."* **James 2:17** reminds us:
- Look for ways to **serve in your church, mentor young believers, or contribute to your local community.**

- **Reflection: How Can You Serve?Be a Voice for Justice**
  - **Standing for truth and righteousness** reflects God's **heart for justice and compassion.**
  - Speak up for those in need, advocate for what is right, and live in a way that reflects Christ's love for the oppressed.
  - *"Act justly and to love mercy and to walk humbly with your God."* **Micah 6:8** calls us to:
  - Whether it's **helping the poor, supporting those in crisis, or working toward fairness and equality,** standing for justice makes a powerful impact.
  - What are some needs in your community that you can help meet?
  - How can your faith be reflected in action this week?
  - What causes or issues is God calling you to stand for?

4. Pray for Future Generations

Prayer is one of the most powerful ways to leave a lasting spiritual legacy. Through prayer, you can **intercede for future generations**, asking God to **guide, protect, and use them for His glory.** Even long after you are gone, the prayers you lift up today **can impact lives for years to come.**

Psalm 145:4 declares:

By faithfully praying for the next generation, you **pass down faith, wisdom, and spiritual covering**, ensuring that God's purposes continue beyond your lifetime.

How to Support Future Generations through Prayer

1. Pray for Their Faith and Spiritual Growth

- Ask God to **draw their hearts toward Him** and deepen their love for His Word.
- Pray for them to be **bold in their faith** and to stand firm in truth.
- *"That Christ may dwell in your hearts through faith. And I pray that you, being rooted and established in love."* **Ephesians 3:17** encourages us to pray:

2. Pray for Their Protection and Guidance

- Ask God to **watch over them, protect them from harm, and lead them in His ways**.
- Pray that they will be **guided by His wisdom** in their decisions and relationships.
- *"Trust in the Lord with all your heart and lean not on your own understanding; in all your ways submit to Him, and He will make your paths straight."* **Proverbs 3:5-6** reminds us to trust in God's direction:

3. Pray for Their Purpose and Calling

- Ask God to **reveal His plan for their lives** and equip them to walk in His purpose.
- Pray that they will **use their gifts and talents for God's glory**.
- *"For I know the plans I have for you, declares the Lord, plans to prosper you and not to harm you, plans to give you hope and a future."* **Jeremiah 29:11** affirms God's plans:

Empowering Your Prayers for Future Generations

- Do you have children, grandchildren, or young believers in your life to pray for?
- How can you make prayer for future generations a consistent

part of your life?

- Will you trust that your prayers today will impact lives beyond your lifetime?

Your prayers have a lasting impact. By lifting up future generations in prayer, you play a crucial role in shaping their faith, safeguarding their journey, and equipping them to confidently follow God's calling. Never underestimate the lasting impact of a life devoted to prayer!

5. Be Faithful in Small Things

Legacy is not built in a single grand gesture—it is formed through small, consistent acts of faithfulness in daily life. Your **kindness, encouragement, and faithfulness in seemingly small acts of obedience** can leave a deep and lasting impact on those around you.

Luke 16:10 reminds us:

The small things, such as showing kindness, handling challenges, and living out your faith, collectively create a legacy that points others to Christ.

Practical Steps for Faithfulness in Small Things:

1. Show Kindness Daily

- A simple act of kindness—a smile, a listening ear, or a word of encouragement—can make a lasting impact.

- *"Clothe yourselves with compassion, kindness, humility, gentleness, and patience."* **Colossians 3:12** encourages us:

2. Speak Encouragement and Truth

- Your words have the power to build up or tear down—choose to speak words of encouragement, faith, and hope into others.
- *"Gracious words are a honeycomb, sweet to the soul and healing to the bones."* **Proverbs 16:24** reminds us:

3. Remain Faithful in Obedience

- Being faithful in **small daily choices** strengthens your character and trust in God.
- Whether **you consistently pray, study Scripture, or follow God's leading**, each step **deepens your faith and sets an example for others.**
- *"Always give yourselves fully to the work of the Lord, because you know that your labor in the Lord is not in vain."* **1 Corinthians 15:58** encourages perseverance:

How do you demonstrate faithfulness in the small things?

- Have you recognized the impact of small acts of kindness and encouragement?

- Are you remaining faithful in daily obedience to God?
- In what ways can you reflect Christ to others in your daily interactions?

Faithfulness in small things leads to a legacy characterized by love, encouragement, and godly influence. By living with consistency and integrity, you leave behind a testimony that inspires others to follow Christ.

1. **1. Mentoring Young People***"And the things you have heard me say in the presence of many witnesses entrust to reliable people who will also be qualified to teach others."* **(NIV)2. Leaving a Written Legacy***"Let this be written for a future generation, that a people not yet created may praise the Lord."* **(NIV)3. Supporting Organizations That Make a Difference***"Whoever is kind to the poor lends to the Lord, and He will reward them for what they have done."* **(NIV)4. Living a Life of Integrity***"The righteous lead blameless lives; blessed are their children after them."* **(NIV)Shaping Your Enduring LegacyPractical Ways to Leave a Legacy of Courageous Faith**

Leaving a legacy of courageous faith means living a purposeful life that reflects God's love and positively impacts others, one life at a time.

Encouragement to Leave a Legacy of Courageous Faith

Your life is significant not just for your achievements, but for the faith you inspire in those around you. You are part of **God's larger story**, and He can use your **testimony, actions, and love** to impact **generations** beyond your own.

Psalm 78:4 reminds us of this sacred responsibility:

Strive for faithfulness as you journey towards leaving a legacy.

Leaving a **legacy of faith** doesn't require perfection. **God works through ordinary, faithful people** who are willing to:

- **Live authentically** – Be real about your struggles and victories in faith.
- **Trust God wholeheartedly** – Walk in obedience, even when the path is uncertain.
- **Share His goodness boldly** – Tell others about His faithfulness in your life.

The faith you nurture today will bear fruit that significantly impacts future generations.

Which step will you take today to make a difference?

- Will you offer a simple act of kindness that reflects Christ's love?

- Will you encourage someone who is struggling in their faith?
- Will you share your testimony to inspire others?

Your life is a testimony, and your faith can inspire a ripple effect that extends beyond your lifetime. Take a step today to build a lasting impact that honors God and encourages others to live courageously for Him.

CONCLUSION: STEPPING FORWARD IN COURAGEOUS FAITH

As you approach the end of this journey, you are invited to live a life of courageous faith. God has a unique purpose for your life, one that requires you to step out in bravery, trust His promises, and rely on His strength. Life may present challenges and uncertainties, but remember that His grace is sufficient, and His love is unending. By walking in faith, you can face each day with confidence, knowing that He is with you every step of the way. Trust in Him, rely on His guidance, and boldly follow the path He has set for you. With God by your side, you can overcome any obstacle and live a life full of purpose, joy, and peace. So as you move forward, may you find strength in His promises and courage in His love to embrace all He has for you. And may your faith continue to grow stronger with each step of the journey. So go forth with grace, forgiveness, and courage knowing that God is always by your side. Keep living out your faith fearlessly, trusting in Him who makes all things possible.

Courageous Faith: A Daily Choice

Courageous faith **is not about being fearless—it's about choosing to trust in a God who is greater than your fears, stronger than your challenges, and faithful in all His ways.** It is about waking up each day and saying, **"Lord, I trust You, even when the path is unclear."**

Throughout this book, we have:

Examined the nature of fear and how faith empowers us to overcome it.

Explored the power of forgiveness and its role in healing and freedom.

Discovered strength in weakness, allowing God to work through our limitations.

Learned to trust God in uncertainty, stepping forward even when the future is unclear.

Cultivated daily acts of bravery, recognizing that small steps of faith shape a bold life.

Recognized the power of community, surrounding ourselves with those who strengthen our faith.

Embraced our ability to leave a lasting legacy, ensuring that our faith impacts future generations.

Now It's Time to Step Forward

This journey has not been about simply learning—it has been about transformation. Faith and courage are a way of life, not just concepts. They call you to action, obedience, and bold trust in God. It's time to take what you've learned and step forward with conviction. Each step of faith draws you closer to Him, aligning your heart with His plans and purposes. Don't wait for perfect circumstances or the absence of fear; take that step, knowing that God's strength is made perfect in your weakness.

Remember, every act of obedience, no matter how small, is significant in God's sight. Even when the steps seem insignificant or unnoticed, they are part of a greater plan.

Example from Scripture:

- When **David obeyed** his father's instruction to deliver food to his brothers (1 Samuel 17:17-20), he **had no idea** that this small act of obedience would lead him to **defeat Goliath and step into his destiny**.

- When the **widow at Zarephath obeyed Elijah** and used her last bit of flour and oil to make him bread (1 Kings 17:8-16), God **miraculously provided for her household** throughout the famine.

Obedience opens doors to God's provision.
Obedience prepares you for greater opportunities.
Obedience is an act of faith that aligns you with His perfect plan.

Step Forward in Faith

Trust **His timing** and **His promises** as you move boldly into what lies ahead. This is **your moment to shine His light**, to **live out your faith authentically**, and to **fulfill the calling He has placed on your life**.

With **God leading the way, the possibilities are limitless. Your obedience today is shaping your future in ways you may not yet see.**

Now is the time—step forward in faith!

What step of faith is God calling you to take?

- **Is it trusting Him in a situation that seems impossible?**
- **Is it letting go of fear and embracing your God-given purpose?**
- **Is it using your testimony to encourage and uplift others?**

Joshua 1:9 reminds us:

Your Time to Rise

Now is your moment to rise. Leave behind doubt and fear. Boldly step into the life God has called you to live. Your identity is not determined by the challenges you face or the mistakes of your past. Instead, you are called to live a life of purpose, rooted in faith and guided by His unfailing love.

- **Embrace faith over fear:** Embrace faith over fear, knowing that God's promises are true even in times of uncertainty. Lean into His word and His strength, for He walks beside you every step of the way. Trust that He is working all things for your good, even when the path ahead seems unclear.
- **Trust God's promises, even in uncertainty:** When uncertainty clouds your path, remember that God's promises remain unshaken. His word is a firm foundation, a rock

upon which you can stand when the ground beneath you feels unstable. Even when life feels unpredictable and you're faced with doubt, trust that He sees the bigger picture and is weaving everything together for a purpose far greater than you can imagine.

- **Live with courage, knowing He is always with you:** Live with courage, confident that He who called you is faithful. The world needs the light that only you can shine—a light born of hope, perseverance, and unwavering trust in God's plan. This is your time to live with courageous faith, to rise above, and to step into the fullness of what God has prepared for you.

The journey doesn't end here—it begins now. Stand firm, take that first step, and walk boldly into the life He has destined for you. With God by your side, there is no limit to what you can achieve. Rise up; it's your time!

A Final Call to Embrace God's Purpose with Bravery

Throughout this book, we've seen how faith empowers ordinary people to do extraordinary things. From the stories of biblical heroes like Abraham, Esther, and Joseph to the quiet, brave moments in our own lives, one truth remains constant: God's purpose for each of us is both powerful and personal. He equips us with courage to step out of our comfort zones and step into a life of obedience and trust. Just as Abraham ventured into the unknown, trusting God's promises, or Esther found the courage to speak up for her people at great personal risk, we too are called to lean into God's purpose even when the path ahead seems unclear.

This is your moment to respond to His call with boldness. Lay aside fear, doubt, and hesitation, and choose to stand on His promises. His strength is displayed in your weakness, and His grace will support you at every step of the journey. Though challenges may arise, and the road may be difficult, God's plan will always prevail. Trust in His unfailing love and take the leap of faith that leads to the extraordinary life He has planned just for you. Now is the time to say "yes" to His purpose with unwavering bravery. This is your moment to illuminate His glory!

God honors those who trust Him enough to take the next step.

Jeremiah 29:11 reminds us:

God's plans for you are good, even when the path feels uncertain. Though the road may twist and turn, and challenges may seem insurmountable, His purpose remains steadfast. Trusting Him in those pivotal moments not only strengthens your faith but also reinforces the assurance that He is working all things together for your good. His guidance and love are unfailing, and as you take each step forward, remember that He is paving the way to fulfill His promises in your life.

A Final Call to Embrace God's Purpose with Bravery

No matter where you are in your walk, the call to step forward in faith is a challenging promise. It requires courage to leave behind the familiar, to face your fears, and to trust that God's plans are greater than your own. Yet, with each step you take, something profound happens—your faith deepens, your strength increases, and God's glory shines through you.

His purpose for your life is uniquely yours, crafted with love and intention. You were designed to make an impact, to live fully in His grace, and to share His light with the world. Will you say "yes" to His call today? Will you be brave enough to move forward, despite the uncertainties?

Remember, God equips the called. He strengthens the weak, uplifts the weary, and guides those who earnestly seek Him. This is your time to rise, to trust, and to pursue His purpose with unwavering bravery. The path may not always be clear, but His promise is sure. Take the next step—He is with you, every step of the way.

Jeremiah 29:11 reassures us of God's divine plan:

Even when the journey feels uncertain, God's plans for you are good. Bravery to move forward despite doubts, bravery to stand firm in the face of challenges, and bravery to trust that He will provide everything you need foster reliance on His faithfulness.

It's not always easy to step into the unknown, yet God never asks you to walk alone. He goes before you, preparing the way and providing the strength you need to persevere. Your courage to keep going, even when the path is unclear, becomes a powerful testimony of faith. And in your surrender, God's power is made perfect, showing you that His promises are always faithful and His plans are always good.

But embracing His purpose **requires bravery**—

- **Bravery to move forward despite doubts is essential for growth and transformation.**

- **Bravery to stand firm in the face of challenges strengthens your character and resolve.**
- **Bravery to trust that He will provide everything you need.**

Your Life Has Meaning and Purpose

No matter what your calling is—whether it's leading a ministry, serving in your community, raising a family, or simply being a light in your workplace—your life holds deep significance.

- **Your story matters.** Someone needs to hear how God has worked in your life. Your struggles, victories, and the ways His love has transformed you are all parts of a testimony that can inspire hope and renewal in someone else.
- **Your faith is an inspiration to others.** Your trust in God can encourage them to step forward in their own journey. When people see your courage to walk in faith—even in difficult times—it can ignite a spark of bravery in their hearts, pushing them toward their purpose in Him.
- **Your actions leave a legacy.** The choices you make today impact future generations. By living a life anchored in God's truths and love, you become a beacon of hope and an example of faithfulness for others. The seeds you plant now can bear fruit long after you're gone, touching lives and advancing God's kingdom in ways you may never fully witness.

A Courageous Step Forward

God is calling you to live **with bold faith**. The question is:

Will you answer the call?

- **Will you step out in faith, even when the road ahead is unclear?**
- **Will you trust God's promises, even when fear tries to hold you back?**
- **Will you live each day as a testimony of His goodness?**

Faith is not the absence of doubt, but the choice to trust God despite it. It's in the moments of uncertainty that faith shines brightest. Each step you take in faith, no matter how small, is a declaration of your trust in His plan for your life. When you respond boldly to His call, you pave the way for His blessings and His purpose to manifest through you.

Remember, bold faith doesn't mean you won't face challenges—it means you'll face them with the confidence that God is with you. Trust in His promises, lean on His strength, and move forward knowing that He goes before you. A courageous step forward in faith may be the very action that leads you to the abundant life He has prepared for you.

Deuteronomy 31:6 encourages us:

This is your moment to embrace God's purpose with courage and conviction. Step forward boldly, knowing that you are never alone—God is with you, guiding you every step of the way. Trust that

He has equipped you with everything you need to fulfill His calling. The path may not always be easy, but it is always worth it. Lean into His wisdom, and allow His Word to be a lamp to your feet and a light to your path. Take heart, for the Creator of the universe is on your side, and with Him, there is no obstacle too great to overcome.

This Is Your Time to Shine

This is your moment—your opportunity to embrace your God-given purpose and step into the fullness of the life He has planned for you. God has uniquely designed you for a purpose that only you can fulfill. His plans for you are intentional and rich with promise, crafted specifically for the gifts and talents He has placed within you.

Now is the time to walk in faith, courage, and boldness, knowing that He is guiding your steps. When you trust in His plan and surrender your fears to Him, you allow His power to work through you in ways you never imagined. This is not the season to hold back or walk in doubt—this is the season to rise in the certainty of His love, His grace, and His wisdom. Step forward, and watch how God will unfold His divine purpose in your life, one step of faith at a time.

Embrace the Journey Ahead

Embrace the Unknown

- **Embrace the uncertainty that awaits you and be willing to venture beyond your comfort zone.**

- True faith **is trusting in God even when you can't see the whole path**.

- *"So do not fear, for I am with you; do not be dismayed, for I am your God. I will strengthen you and help you; I will uphold you with my righteous right hand."* **(NIV)Isaiah 41:10** reminds us:

Trust in God's Guidance

- **Surrender your anxieties** and trust in God's **perfect timing and plan**.
- Even when things don't go as expected, **He is working behind the scenes for your good.**
- *"Trust in the Lord with all your heart and lean not on your own understanding; in all your ways submit to Him, and He will make your paths straight."* **Proverbs 3:5-6** encourages us:

Live a Life of Purpose

- **Use your unique gifts and talents** to serve others and **make a difference in the world**.
- You were **created for more than just existing—you were made to impact lives!**
- *"For we are God's handiwork, created in Christ Jesus to do good works, which God prepared in advance for us to do."* **Ephesi ans 2:10** declares:

Never Stop Growing

- **Deepen your faith**, expand your horizons, and strive to become **the best version of yourself**.
- Growth requires **commitment and courage**, but God will **equip you for every step.**

- *"Being confident of this, that He who began a good work in you will carry it on to completion until the day of Christ Jesus."***P hilippians 1:6** assures us:

Your Time Is Now

What step of faith will you take today?
Where is God calling you to step out with courage?
How can you use your gifts to glorify Him and bless others?

Embrace this moment to shine brightly. Step boldly into God's purpose, trust His guidance, and walk in faith—anticipating the best that is yet to come!

Faith Equips Us to Face Life's Challenges

Life is unpredictable. Challenges will come, doubts will arise, and fear will whisper that you're not enough. But as a child of God, you are never alone. His presence surrounds you in every trial, and His strength is made perfect in your weakness. When the weight of uncertainty feels overwhelming, remember that God's promises are your anchor. He has promised to never leave you nor forsake you, and His peace surpasses all understanding, guarding your heart and mind in Christ Jesus (Deuteronomy 31:8; Hebrews 13:5; Philippians 4:7).

Lean into His Word when doubt creeps in and fear attempts to take hold. Meditate on His truth and draw strength from His unchanging character. With God by your side, you are equipped to face whatever comes your way. Remember, He has not given you a spirit of fear, but of power, love, and a sound mind. Trust in His unfailing love, for

He is always faithful to guide you through even the most uncertain moments of life.

Faith equips you with everything you need to overcome obstacles and walk in **victory.**

Isaiah 41:10 offers this powerful assurance:

God's Presence, Power, and Promises Sustain You

When you feel weak, His strength is sufficient. God does not expect us to rely on our own power—**He strengthens us when we have nothing left to give.**

Example from Scripture:

- *"My grace is sufficient for you, for My power is made perfect in weakness."*

  2 Corinthians 12:9 (NIV)Paul's Thorn in the Flesh: The Apostle Paul struggled with a persistent weakness, but instead of removing it, God reassured him:

Paul realized that

his weakness was not a limitation but an opportunity for God's power to be displayed.

- **Gideon's Small Army:** Gideon felt unqualified and weak when God called him to **defeat the Midianites**. But God reduced his army from **32,000 men to just 300** so that victory would come **not from human strength, but through God's power (Judges 7:2-7)**.

When you feel unqualified, God equips you.
When you feel overwhelmed, He sustains you.
When you feel inadequate, He reminds you that His power is at work in you.

Lean on His Strength

No matter what challenges you face, **you don't have to carry them alone. God's strength is limitless, and He will uphold you when you feel weak.**

Isaiah 40:29 promises:

When you feel weak, trust that God's strength is more than enough to carry you through.

When you feel unsure, His Word lights your path.

- *"Your word is a lamp to my feet, a light on my path."* **Psalm 119:105** declares:

When you feel overwhelmed, His peace guards your heart.

- *"Do not be anxious about anything, but in every situation, by prayer and petition, with thanksgiving, present your requests to God. And the peace of God, which transcends all understanding, will guard your hearts and your minds in Christ Jesus."* **Philippians 4:6-7** encourages:

You Don't Have to Muster Courage on Your Own

You have the Spirit of God to lead, empower, and uphold you. You don't have to face life's uncertainties alone—His strength is actively working in you.

Ephesians 3:20 declares:

You are fully equipped to conquer any challenge

Whatever lies ahead, **God has already given you everything you need** to face it.

What challenge are you facing today?
Where do you need to lean on His strength instead of your own?
How can you walk forward in faith, trusting that He is leading the way?

In Him, you find strength, all you need, and victory. Step forward with unwavering faith, knowing that God is by your side, and His faithfulness is steadfast!

You Are Not Alone on This Journey

Remember, you are never alone. No matter what challenges you face, **God is with you every step of the way**, providing the **strength, courage, and guidance** you need.

Jesus reassures us in Matthew 28:20:

When life feels overwhelming, when uncertainty clouds your path, or when fear tries to take hold—**hold fast to the truth that God's presence is constant.** He never leaves you, and His power is always at work in your life.

Isaiah 40:29 reminds us of His strength:

God Is Your Strength and Refuge

When you feel weak, He strengthens you. When you feel weak, God strengthens you. In times of exhaustion, discouragement, or overwhelming challenges, **God provides the strength you need to endure and overcome.** He does not expect you to rely on your own power—**His strength is made perfect in your weakness.**

Examples from Scripture:

- *"But He said to me, 'My grace is sufficient for you, for My power is made perfect in weakness.' Therefore I will boast all the more gladly about my weaknesses, so that Christ's power may rest on me."*
  2 Corinthians 12:9 (NIV)Paul's Weakness Became His Strength:
  Paul struggled with a personal weakness—one he pleaded with God to remove. **Instead of taking it away, God reassured him that His grace was enough.**

God's strength isn't just given to you—it works through you.

- *"He gives strength to the weary and increases the power of*

the weak. Even youths grow tired and weary, and young men stumble and fall; but those who hope in the Lord will renew their strength. They will soar on wings like eagles; they will run and not grow weary, they will walk and not be faint."
Isaiah 40:29-31 (NIV)

Strength for the Weary: Life's burdens can drain you, but **God renews the strength of those who trust in Him.**

- *"I can do all things through Christ who strengthens me."* **Philippians 4:13 (NKJV)God's Strength in Every Challenge:**
  When you face obstacles that seem impossible, **God's presence empowers you to keep moving forward.**

Rely on His Strength

When you feel physically, emotionally, or spiritually drained, turn to Him for renewal.

When challenges seem too big, remember that His strength carries you.

When you don't feel strong enough, trust that His power is working within you.

Your weakness is not a limitation—it is an invitation for God's strength to be revealed. Trust in Him, and He will uphold you!

When you feel lost, He guides you. In seasons of uncertainty, confusion, or doubt, **God provides direction, clarity, and purpose.** He never leaves us wandering aimlessly—**He leads us step by step, even when we can't see the whole path.**

Examples from Scripture:

- **The Israelites in the Wilderness:**
  After leaving Egypt, the Israelites **didn't know the way to the Promised Land**, but **God led them** with a **pillar of cloud by day and a pillar of fire by night** (**Exodus 13:21-22**). Even in the wilderness, **God provided guidance every step of the way.**

- *"The Lord is my shepherd, I lack nothing. He makes me lie down in green pastures, He leads me beside quiet waters, He refreshes my soul. He guides me along the right paths for His name's sake."*
  Psalm 23:1-3 (NIV)Psalm 23: The Lord as Our Shepherd:
  Just as a shepherd leads his sheep, **God gently leads us, protects us, and restores us** when we feel lost.

- *"I am the light of the world. Whoever follows me will never walk in darkness but will have the light of life."*
  John 8:12 (NIV) Jesus as the Light of the World:
  When we don't know where to go, **Jesus is our light in the darkness.** He promises to guide us if we follow Him:

Trust in His Guidance

When you feel unsure about your next step, seek Him in prayer.
When life feels overwhelming, trust that His Word will illuminate your path.
Even when you don't see the full picture, God is leading you one step at a time.

Proverbs 3:5-6 reassures us:

You may feel lost, but God knows exactly where you are—and He will always guide you forward.

When you feel afraid, He reassures you. When you feel afraid, God reassures you. Fear is a natural response to uncertainty, danger, or the unknown, but **God's presence brings peace and confidence even in the most difficult moments.**

Examples from Scripture:

- *"But Jesus immediately said to them: "Take courage! It is I. Don't be afraid.'"*

  Matthew 14:27 (NIV) Jesus Calming the Storm:
  The disciples were terrified when a violent storm threatened their boat. **Jesus reassured them with His presence and authority, calming both the storm and their fears.**

- *"Have I not commanded you? Be strong and courageous. Do not be afraid; do not be discouraged, for the Lord your God will be with you wherever you go."*

  Joshua 1:9 (NIV)God's Assurance to Joshua:
  As Joshua stepped into leadership after Moses, he likely felt overwhelmed by the responsibility. **God reassured him that he was not alone.**

- *"So do not fear, for I am with you; do not be dismayed, for I am your God. I will strengthen you and help you; I will uphold you with my righteous right hand."*

  Isaiah 41:10 (NIV):

God's Presence in Our Fear: No matter what fear we face, **God promises to uphold us and strengthen us.**

Trust in His Reassurance

When fear overwhelms you, remember that God is with you.
When doubts creep in, cling to His promises of protection and peace.
When life feels uncertain, rest in the assurance that He is in control.

Fear may come, but God's reassurance is greater. In His presence, you will always find peace.

These verses **offer profound reassurance**, reminding us that **we can face any obstacle with confidence, knowing that God is our strength and refuge.**

You don't walk this journey alone.
God's presence goes before you, walks beside you, and upholds you.
With Him, you have the strength to overcome, the courage to persevere, and the faith to walk boldly into His plans.

Step forward with confidence, knowing that God is with you, now and always!

A Personalized Prayer of Commitment to Courageous Faith

Heavenly Father,

I come before You with a heart open to Your will and a spirit ready to walk in faith. Thank You for Your unwavering presence, Your boundless love, and the strength You provide in every season of life.

Lord, I surrender my fears, doubts, and uncertainties to You. I choose to trust in Your perfect plan, even when the path ahead is unclear. Help me to step forward with boldness, knowing that You go before me, walk beside me, and uphold me with Your mighty hand.

Fill me with courage to embrace the unknown, faith to believe in Your promises, and perseverance to remain steadfast in every trial. When fear whispers that I am not enough, remind me that **You are my strength, my refuge, and my ever-present help in times of need**.

Father, use my life to glorify You. Let my words, actions, and choices reflect Your goodness and love. May I be a light in the darkness, a vessel of Your grace, and an instrument of encouragement to those around me.

I commit my journey to You, Lord. Lead me where You desire, and give me the courage to follow. No matter what comes my way, I will stand firm in faith, knowing that You are always with me.

In Jesus' name, I pray,

Amen.

This is your moment to commit to a life of courageous faith. Step forward boldly, trusting in **God's strength, wisdom, and unfailing love.** He has called you, and He will equip you for everything ahead!

A Prayer for Courageous Faith

Heavenly Father,

Thank You for calling me to live a life of **purpose and faith**. I acknowledge that **I am weak on my own**, but in You, I am strong. Today, I surrender my fears, doubts, and insecurities to You, trusting Your guidance every step of the way.

Lord, help me to walk boldly in obedience, even when the path is unclear. Teach me to trust Your promises and wisdom and to find rest in Your presence. Fill my heart with **courage to face challenges, grace to overcome failures, and perseverance to fulfill Your calling on my life.**

May my life reflect Your love, testify to Your faithfulness, and be a beacon of hope to those around me. **Use me, Lord, to inspire others to boldly live for You, so that my words and actions may lead them closer to Your truth.**

Today, I choose to step forward in faith, believing You will provide, protect, and lead me. I commit my life to You, knowing that **Your plans are greater than anything I could ever imagine.**

In Jesus' name, I pray. Amen.

Step forward with faith today, knowing that God's unwavering presence and guidance will empower you for every step ahead.

A Declaration for Courageous Faith

As I move forward, I declare:

I will live with courageous faith, trusting in God's plans and promises even when the path is uncertain.

I will embrace my purpose, standing firm in trials and relying on His strength to guide me.

I will leave a legacy of hope, love, and boldness, inspiring others to walk in faith.

With God by my side, **I will not live in fear**—I will walk in confidence, knowing that **He is my strength and my refuge.**

Today, I step forward in courageous faith.

A Prayer of Commitment

Lord, I commit to living a life of courageous faith.
Help me overcome my fears, trust in Your guidance, and step into the fullness of Your purpose for my life.
Grant me the courage to embrace the unknown, to serve others with love and boldness, and to leave a lasting legacy of faith and hope.
May my life reflect Your light, my words bring encouragement, and my actions inspire others to trust in You.

In Jesus' name, Amen.

Make this your daily declaration—step forward with faith, knowing God leads the way!

Moving Forward

You are just beginning your journey of courageous faith. Each day presents an opportunity to **take small, bold steps**, trusting that **God is leading you**.

When fear arises, remember His promises.
When challenges come, lean into His strength.
When victories are won, give Him the glory.

You are not here by accident—you are called, chosen, and equipped by God for a specific purpose, ready to make a meaningful difference in the world.

God has designed you for **a life of meaning and purpose**. You are not here by accident—**you are called, chosen, and equipped** to make a difference. **With God, everything is possible.**

Deuteronomy 31:8 reminds us:

Step Forward in Faith

Step forward with courage, knowing God goes before you, walks beside you, and carries you through every season of life.
The world needs your light, so shine brightly!
Live boldly and embrace the incredible journey God has planned for you.

Take Action Now

This is not just a conclusion—it is an invitation to embrace a life of purpose, a life lived in courageous faith. Step into each day with the assurance that the Creator of the universe walks beside you. Choose to trust His plan even when the path ahead seems unclear. Surrender your fears, doubts, and anxieties into His capable hands, and allow Him to work all things for your good.

The world needs the light that only you can bring, a light that reflects the love, hope, and joy found in Christ. May you go forth with boldness, faith, and unwavering trust, knowing that God is with you every step of the way. You are called, empowered, and loved—now is the time to live out your faith without hesitation and make an eternal impact.

Now is the time to embark on your journey—live courageously and boldly, shining your light in the world!

BONUS SECTION: TOOLS FOR CULTIVATING COURAGEOUS FAITH

DEEPENING YOUR JOURNEY IN COURAGEOUS FAITH

Embark on a transformative journey to deepen your understanding, reflect on your path, and empower yourself to cultivate unwavering, courageous faith with this bonus section. Through **reflection questions, a 30-day challenge, and recommended Scriptures**, you'll have the tools to **live boldly and confidently embrace God's calling.**

Reflection Questions and Exercises for Each Chapter

Chapter 1: What is Courageous Faith?

Courageous faith is more than just bravery—it is a deep, unwavering trust in God, even in the face of fear, uncertainty, or adversity. It is the willingness to step out in obedience, knowing that God is in control, even when we cannot see the full picture.

Reflection Questions:

How do you define courageous faith in your own words?

- How does it differ from simple bravery?

Which biblical example of faith inspires you the most, and why?

- Consider figures like Abraham, Moses, Esther, Peter, or Paul. What can you learn from their faith journey?

What small act of faith can you take this week to demonstrate trust in God?

- Is there a conversation you need to have, a step you need to take, or a fear you need to surrender?

Share a personal story where you witnessed or experienced courageous faith in action.

- Was there a time when you (or someone you know) trusted God despite uncertainty? What was the outcome?

What does it mean to you to "live a life less ordinary"?

- How does faith push you beyond your comfort zone and into a life of purpose?

Exercise: Stepping Out in Faith

Write down an area of your life where you feel God is calling you to step out in faith.

- This could be in your career, relationships, ministry, or personal growth.

Pray specifically for courage and clarity in that area.

- Ask God to remove fear, strengthen your trust, and give you wisdom for the next step.

Living a Life Less Ordinary

Living a life less ordinary means constantly seeking **opportunities to grow and serve others**, even when it feels **uncomfortable or uncertain**. It means:

Choosing faith over fear.

Trusting God's plan over personal comfort.

Saying "yes" to His calling, even when it feels risky.

Walking in obedience, knowing that He will equip you.

True courageous faith is not just about big moments—it is about daily obedience, trusting God in both the ordinary and extraordinary.

Final Thought:

What is one way you can **live boldly in faith this week?** Write it down and commit to taking that step!

Chapter 2: Fear and Faith – A Balancing Act

Fear and faith often coexist, but **true courageous faith chooses to trust God despite fear.** When we allow fear to dictate our choices, we miss out on the fullness of God's plan. But when we **submit our**

fears to Him, we can walk forward in confidence, knowing that He is with us.

Reflection Questions:

What fears are currently holding you back from fully trusting God?

- Are they related to failure, rejection, uncertainty, or something else?

How has God helped you overcome fear in the past?

- Reflect on a time when you were afraid, but God came through for you.

Which Scripture about overcoming fear resonates most with you?

- Examples:
    - *Isaiah 41:10 – "Do not fear, for I am with you."*
    - *2 Timothy 1:7 – "For God has not given us a spirit of fear, but of power, love, and a sound mind."*

Identify a specific fear that is holding you back. What are the root causes of this fear?

- Is it past experiences, self-doubt, or a lack of trust in God's plan?

Write down three truth-based affirmations to counter your fear.

- Example: Instead of *"I'm not strong enough"*, declare *"God's strength is made perfect in my weakness" (2 Corinthians 12:9).*

How can you cultivate a more positive and encouraging inner dialogue?

- What steps can you take to replace fearful thoughts with faith-filled ones?

Exercise: Overcoming Fear with God's Promises

List three promises from Scripture that counteract your fears.

- Examples:
  - *Joshua 1:9 – "Be strong and courageous... for the Lord your God will be with you wherever you go."*
  - *Philippians 4:6-7 – "Do not be anxious about anything... and the peace of God will guard your hearts and minds."*
  - *Psalm 56:3 – "When I am afraid, I put my trust in You."*

Post these verses somewhere visible (mirror, phone screen, journal) so you can be reminded of God's truth daily.

Choosing Faith Over Fear

Fear may whisper, but faith must speak louder.
Fear may feel powerful, but God's promises are greater.
Fear may linger, but you can move forward anyway.

What small act of faith will you take today to trust God more than your fears? Write it down and step into His peace!

Chapter 3: Faith in Action

Faith is more than **belief**—it requires **action**. **True faith moves forward**, even when the outcome is uncertain. God calls us to step out in obedience, trusting that He will guide and provide along the way.

Reflection Questions:

Identify a specific area in your life where you are being called to step out in faith.

- What is the **first step** you can take today?

How do you typically respond when faced with uncertainty?

- Do you hesitate, worry, or seek control? How can you shift your response to **trusting God more?**

How does the story of Noah, Abraham, or another biblical figure challenge or encourage you?

- **Noah:** Built an ark in obedience, even before the flood came (*Genesis 6-7*).
- **Abraham:** Left his homeland without knowing where God was leading (*Hebrews 11:8*).
- **Peter:** Walked on water toward Jesus but began to sink when he doubted (*Matthew 14:29-31*).
- What lessons can you apply to your own faith journey?

Reflect on a time when you experienced God's faithfulness in response to your obedience.

- Did He provide, open a door, or guide you in ways you didn't expect?

How can you better discern God's will for your life?

- What steps can you take to hear His voice more clearly through **prayer, Scripture, and wise counsel**?

Exercise: Taking Faith into Action

Take one small step of faith this week.

- Ideas:

  Reach out to someone you feel led to encourage.

  Start a project God has placed on your heart.

  Say "yes" to an opportunity that scares you.

  Let go of a fear or habit that holds you back.

Faith grows through action. Even small steps create **momentum and deepen trust in God's plan.**

Faith in Action Starts Today

Faith isn't just something we believe—it's something we live.
Faith requires stepping out, even before we see the full picture.
Faith trusts that God's plans are greater than our own.

What step of faith will you take today? Write it down and commit to acting on it!

Chapter 4: Navigating Pain and Forgiveness

Forgiveness is one of the **hardest yet most freeing** acts of faith. **Holding onto bitterness keeps us bound, but releasing it through forgiveness brings healing.** True forgiveness does not excuse wrongdoing but allows **God's grace** to work in us and through us.

Reflection Questions:

Who do you need to forgive, and what steps can you take to begin the process?

- Is it a past hurt, a broken relationship, or even **forgiving yourself**?

Identify a situation or relationship where you need to extend forgiveness.

- What are the obstacles preventing you from forgiving? **Fear, pride, pain, or a sense of injustice?**

How has unforgiveness affected your spiritual growth or relationships?

- Have you felt **distant from God**, struggled with trust, or carried emotional burdens?

What can Joseph's story teach you about trusting God's plan even through pain?

- *"You intended to harm me, but God intended it for good."* **(Genesis 50:20)Joseph was betrayed by his brothers** yet later forgave them, saying:

- How does this perspective change your view of **pain and purpose**?

How can you practice self-compassion in your own healing journey?

- Are you holding onto guilt or shame? **God's grace covers**

you, too.

What does it mean to you to truly forgive?

- How can you **cultivate a spirit of forgiveness** in your daily life?

Exercise: Releasing Through a Letter

Write a letter to someone you need to forgive.

- **You don't have to send it.**
- Express your pain, release bitterness, and **surrender the situation to God**.
- End with a prayer, asking God to **heal your heart** and help you walk in freedom.

Choosing Forgiveness Brings Healing

Forgiveness doesn't mean forgetting—it means choosing peace over resentment.
Letting go doesn't minimize the pain—it maximizes God's power to heal.
Forgiveness is a gift you give yourself, allowing you to move forward in freedom.

What step will you take today to release bitterness and embrace healing? Write it down and begin the journey to **freedom through forgiveness.**

Chapter 5: Finding Strength in Weakness

The world teaches us to hide our weaknesses, but **God's power is most visible in our places of struggle**. When we acknowledge our weaknesses, **we create space for God to work through us** and display **His strength**.

2 Corinthians 12:9 – *"But He said to me, 'My grace is sufficient for you, for My power is made perfect in weakness.' Therefore I will boast all the more gladly about my weaknesses, so that Christ's power may rest on me."*

Reflection Questions:

Identify a specific weakness that you struggle with.

- How can you view this weakness as an **opportunity** for God to demonstrate His strength?

How have you seen God's strength made perfect in your life?

- Recall a time when you felt **incapable or unqualified**, yet God equipped and sustained you.

How does 2 Corinthians 12:9 encourage you in your struggles?

- What does it mean for **God's grace to be sufficient** in your life?

Read and reflect on 2 Corinthians 12:9.

- How does this verse **challenge your understanding of strength**?

- Instead of trying to be self-sufficient, how can you **lean into God's power?**

How can you learn to embrace your vulnerabilities and share them with trusted others?

- How can sharing your struggles **strengthen relationships** and encourage others?

Exercise: Reflecting on God's Strength

Think of a time when you felt weak but experienced God's strength.

- Did He **provide wisdom, courage, comfort, or guidance?**

- How did He **carry you through** that situation?

Write it down and thank God for His faithfulness.

- Keep this reflection as a **reminder** that **God is always working, even in your weakest moments.**

Embracing God's Strength in Your Weakness

Your weakness is not a limitation—it is an invitation for God's power.
God's grace is enough for you, no matter what you face.
True strength is found in surrender, not self-sufficiency.

What weakness will you surrender to God today? Let Him work through you in **ways beyond your imagination!** Allow Him to show His strength in your weakness.

Chapter 6: Facing Uncertainty with Faith

Uncertainty is a natural part of life, but **faith gives us the courage to trust God even when we don't have all the answers**. Just as God led His people through the wilderness, **He is leading you today.**

Proverbs 3:5-6 – *"Trust in the Lord with all your heart and lean not on your own understanding; in all your ways submit to Him, and He will make your paths straight."*

Reflection Questions:

Identify a current situation in your life where you are experiencing uncertainty.

- What steps can you take to **cultivate trust in God** during this time?

How does the Israelites' journey through the wilderness mirror your own faith journey?

- Have you ever felt **lost, impatient, or unsure of God's plan**?
- How has God **provided for and guided you**, even when the path was unclear?

What spiritual practices help you trust God during uncertain times?

- Do you turn to **prayer, worship, Scripture, fasting, or community for strength?**

Reflect on a time when you experienced God's faithfulness in the midst of uncertainty.

- What did you **learn about His character** during that season?

How can you silence the voice of doubt and replace it with the voice of faith?

- What **Bible verses, prayers, or affirmations** can help you replace fear with faith?

Exercise: Surrendering Uncertainty to God

Spend time in prayer, surrendering your uncertainties to God.

- Be **honest about your fears, doubts, and struggles.**
- Ask for **wisdom, peace, and clarity.**

Journal about what you feel God is teaching you through this season.

- Write about **lessons you are learning** and how God is **shaping your faith** through uncertainty.

Trusting God Even When the Path is Unclear

You don't have to see the whole path—just take the next step in faith.
God's guidance is always present, even if it doesn't look the way you expect.
Faith is trusting that God is working, even when you can't see it.

What area of uncertainty will you surrender to God today? Let go of fear and **walk forward in trust!**

Chapter 7: Cultivating Daily Brave Moments

Bravery isn't just about big, life-changing moments—it's about the **small, daily decisions** to trust God, step outside your comfort zone, and live with faith. **Courage is built through consistency, one step at a time.**

Zechariah 4:10 – *"Do not despise these small beginnings, for the Lord rejoices to see the work begin."*

Reflection Questions:

Identify one small, courageous act you can commit to doing today.

- It could be **starting a difficult conversation, standing up for truth, or stepping into a new opportunity.**

How can journaling or reflecting on past victories strengthen your courage?

- Have you ever been afraid, but then saw God come through?
- How can remembering past victories **increase your faith for future challenges**?

Begin a journal to record your daily acts of courage.

- What **simple or bold steps** have you taken today that required faith?

What prevents you from embracing daily bravery?

- Is it **fear of failure, perfectionism, or self-doubt**?
- How can you take **intentional steps to overcome these obstacles**?

How can you cultivate a more courageous mindset in your everyday life?

- What **Scriptures, affirmations, or habits** can help you build bravery into your daily routine?

Exercise: Start a "Brave Moments" Journal

Each day, write down one act of courage or faith you took, no matter how small.

- It could be:

  Speaking up when it was easier to stay silent.
  Praying for someone even when you felt nervous.
  Taking the first step toward a big goal.
  Choosing faith over fear in a difficult situation.

Review your journal weekly and thank God for how He is growing your faith.

Bravery is Built Daily

Courage is not a one-time event—it's a habit.
God strengthens you as you take small steps of obedience.
Each act of faith prepares you for even greater moments of boldness.

What brave step will you take today? Start small, stay consistent, and watch **how courage becomes a lifestyle!**

Chapter 8: The Power of Community in Faith

Faith is not meant to be lived in isolation. **God designed us to grow, learn, and find strength within a faith community.** Encouragement, accountability, and support from others help us walk boldly in our calling and remain steadfast in our faith.

Hebrews 10:24-25 – *"And let us consider how we may spur one another on toward love and good deeds, not giving up meeting together, as some are in the habit of doing, but encouraging one another—and all the more as you see the Day approaching."*

Reflection Questions:

Who in your life inspires you to live courageously?

- Think about a **mentor, friend, family member, or church leader** whose faith encourages you.

How can you intentionally build a circle of accountability and support?

- What steps can you take to **connect with others who challenge and encourage your faith?**

What role has mentorship or fellowship played in your faith journey?

- Have you been guided or strengthened by a **mentor, Bible study group, or close friend in faith?**
- How has this helped you grow?

How can you strengthen your connections within your faith community?

- Are there **ministries, small groups, or church events** you can get involved in?

- How can you **be more intentional about forming deeper relationships**?

Identify someone in your life who could benefit from your encouragement and support.

- Is there someone **struggling in their faith, facing a challenge, or in need of a kind word?**

How can you cultivate a more supportive and encouraging environment within your community?

- How can you **become a source of encouragement** to those around you?

Exercise: Express Gratitude for Your Faith Community

Reach out to someone who has impacted your faith journey.

- Send a text, make a call, or write a note to **thank them for their influence on your walk with God.**

- Share **how they have inspired or supported you.**

The Strength of Community

You grow stronger when you surround yourself with people who uplift and challenge you.
Your faith can encourage and inspire others just as theirs has encouraged you.
Faith is best lived out in connection with others who push you closer to Christ.

Who will you encourage today? Take a step toward **building deeper faith-filled relationships!**

Chapter 9: Leaving a Legacy of Courageous Faith

Your life is not just about the moments you live but about **the impact you leave behind**. A legacy of courageous faith **inspires, strengthens, and encourages future generations** to trust God, live boldly, and walk in obedience.

Psalm 78:4—"We *will not hide them from their descendants; we will tell the next generation the praiseworthy deeds of the Lord, His power, and the wonders He has done."*

Reflection Questions:

What kind of legacy do you want to leave for future generations?

- How do you want to be **remembered in faith, character, and purpose**?

How can your testimony inspire others to trust God?

- Who might be encouraged by hearing **how God has worked in your life**?

What practical steps can you take today to build a legacy of faith?

- Are there **habits, disciplines, or traditions** you can start that will leave a lasting impact?

How can you use your unique gifts and talents to make a positive impact on the world?

- What strengths or passions can you use to **serve others and glorify God**?

What steps can you take to ensure that your impact is lasting and meaningful?

- How can you **invest in others, mentor, or create something that outlives you**?

Identify one specific action you can take today to begin living a life that reflects your values and beliefs.

- What is one **decision, action, or conversation** you can have today to align your life with your faith?

Exercise: Share Your Faith Story

Write a letter or record a video sharing your faith story and the lessons you've learned.

- **Talk about God's faithfulness, challenges you've overcome, and what you want to pass on to others.**

- Consider **sharing it with loved ones** or **saving it for future generations** as part of your faith legacy.

Your Faith Legacy Starts Today

Every action you take today is shaping the faith of those around you.
Your story can inspire, encourage, and lead others toward God.
A legacy of courageous faith is built through consistent obedience and love.

What step will you take today to leave a lasting impact? Your faith matters—**live boldly and inspire others for generations to come!**

30-Day Courageous Faith Challenge

This 30-day challenge provides daily prompts to help you grow in faith and courage. Focus on the prompt each day and ask God to guide you as you take bold steps forward.

Week 1: Overcoming Fear

Day 1: Write down your biggest fears and surrender them to God in prayer.

Day 2: Memorize Isaiah 41:10 and meditate on it throughout the day.

Day 3: Take one action that confronts a fear, trusting God to guide you.

Day 4: Reflect on a past fear God helped you overcome.

Day 5: Share a Scripture or word of encouragement with someone who may be struggling with fear.

Day 6: Spend 10 minutes in silent prayer, asking God to replace your fear with peace.

Day 7: Write a prayer of gratitude for God's faithfulness in your life.

Week 2: Faith in Action

Day 8: Identify one area of your life where God is calling you to step out in faith.

Day 9: Take one small step of obedience today.

Day 10: Reflect on how Noah or Abraham demonstrated faith in action.

Day 11: Write down three goals that require courageous faith.

Day 12: Spend time praying for clarity and guidance in your next steps.

Day 13: Encourage someone else to act boldly in their faith.

Day 14: Celebrate a recent step of faith you've taken.

Week 3: Building Community

Day 15: Reach out to someone you trust and share a prayer request.

Day 16: Pray for your family, friends, and community.

Day 17: Write down three ways you can support others in their faith journey.

Day 18: Join or commit to attending a small group or Bible study.

Day 19: Reflect on a relationship that has strengthened your faith.

Day 20: Reach out to a mentor or someone who inspires you spiritually.

Day 21: Plan a way to serve or bless someone in your community.

Week 4: Leaving a Legacy

Day 22: Reflect on what legacy you want to leave for future generations.

Day 23: Write down your testimony and pray about sharing it.

Day 24: Start a gratitude journal for answered prayers and God's faithfulness.

Day 25: Pray for wisdom to live in a way that inspires others.

Day 26: Share your faith story with someone who needs encouragement.

Day 27: Write a prayer for your children, family, or future generations.

Day 28: Reflect on Psalm 78:4 and how you can proclaim God's works to others.

Day 29: Thank God for how He has used your life so far.

Day 30: Commit to continuing the journey of courageous faith with God.

Recommended Scriptures for Strength and Courage

- **Joshua 1:9**: *"Have I not commanded you? Be strong and courageous. Do not be afraid; do not be discouraged, for the Lord your God will be with you wherever you go."*

- **Isaiah 41:10**: *"So do not fear, for I am with you; do not be dismayed, for I am your God. I will strengthen you and help you; I will uphold you with my righteous right hand."*

- **Psalm 23:4**: *"Even though I walk through the darkest valley, I will fear no evil, for you are with me; your rod and your staff, they comfort me."*

- **Philippians 4:13**: *"I can do all things through Christ who strengthens me."*

- **Romans 8:28**: *"And we know that in all things God works for the good of those who love Him, who have been called according to His purpose."*

- **2 Corinthians 12:9**: *"But He said to me, 'My grace is sufficient for you, for my power is made perfect in weakness.'"*

- **Psalm 46:1**: *"God is our refuge and strength, an ever-present help in trouble."*

- **Psalm 27:1:** "The Lord is my light and my salvation—whom shall I fear? The Lord is the stronghold of my life—of whom shall I be afraid?"

- **1 Peter 5:7:** "Cast all your anxiety on him because he cares for you."

- **Hebrews 13:5-6:** "Keep your lives free from the love of

> money and be content with what you have, because God has said, 'Never will I leave you; never will I forsake you.'"

Final Encouragement

Remember, building courageous faith is not something you do alone. God's Spirit is with you, empowering you with strength and love every step of the way. Approach this bonus section with an open heart, seeking His guidance as you pursue a life fully surrendered to His will. Allow this time of intentional reflection and action to draw you closer to Him and give you confidence to fulfill His calling on your life. You were created for this.

Living Boldly with Courageous Faith

This bonus section equips you to reflect, act, and grow in courageous faith. It empowers you to live boldly and inspires others to do the same. Step forward with confidence, knowing that God is with you every step of the way. Within this section, you'll find practical exercises, reflective prompts, and actionable challenges designed to deepen your understanding and application of the principles presented in this book.

Take this opportunity to assess where you are in your faith journey and where God is calling you to go. Personalize these exercises to fit your unique circumstances and needs. Whether through prayer, service, or simply stepping outside your comfort zone, use these tools to strengthen your faith and encourage others as you live out your unique purpose in Christ. May God bless you abundantly as you embark on this journey of courageous faith! Stay strong and courageous, for the

Lord your God is with you wherever you go (Joshua 1:9). Remember, YOU are called to make a difference in this world—let your faith be the guiding light that leads others to Him.

Are You Ready?

Are you ready to embrace a life of courageous faith? Are you ready to trust in God's unchanging character and walk boldly into His plans for your life? Are you ready to shine as a light in the darkness, showing others what it means to have unwavering trust in the One who holds all things together?

REFERENCES

Hamilton, B. (2014). *Body and Soul: A Girl's Guide to a Fit, Fun, and Fabulous Life.* Zondervan.

Hamilton, B. (2004). *Soul Surfer: A True Story of Faith, Family, and Fighting to Get Back on the Board.* MTV Books.

Lewis, C. S. (1940). *The Problem of Pain.* HarperOne.

Lewis, C. S. (1952). *Mere Christianity.* HarperOne.

Lutzer, E. (2015). *When a Nation Forgets God: 7 Lessons We Must Learn from Nazi Germany.* Moody Publishers.

Pinkney, A. D. (2000). *Wilma Unlimited: How Wilma Rudolph Became the World's Fastest Woman.* Houghton Mifflin Harcourt.

Rudolph, W. (1977). *Wilma: The Story of Wilma Rudolph.* New American Library.

Tada, J. E. (2006). *Joni: An Unforgettable Story.* Zondervan.

Tada, J. E. (2010). *A Place of Healing: Wrestling with the Mysteries of Suffering, Pain, and God's Sovereignty.* David C Cook.

ten Boom, C., Sherrill, J., & Sherrill, E. (1971). *The Hiding Place.* Chosen Books.

Vujicic, N. (2012). *Unstoppable: The Incredible Power of Faith in Action.* WaterBrook Press.

Vujicic, N. (2010). *Life Without Limits: Inspiration for a Ridiculously Good Life.* WaterBrook Press.

New International Version (NIV). Holy Bible. Biblica, 1973, 1978, 1984, 2011.

New International Version (NIV). Holy Bible. Biblica, 2011. Accessed from Bible Gateway

King James Version (KJV). Holy Bible. Originally published in 1611, public domain.

King James Version (KJV). Holy Bible. 1611. Accessed from Bible Gateway

English Standard Version (ESV). Holy Bible. Copyright © 2001, Crossway, a publishing ministry of Good News Publishers.

Holy Bible, New Living Translation. Tyndale House Publishers. Carol Stream, IL: Tyndale House Publishers, 2015.

Additional Resources:

- "Fearless: Imagine Your Life Without Fear" by Max Lucado
- "Trusting God: Even When Life Hurts" by Jerry Bridges
- "Let Go of Your Fear and Live Again" by Creflo Dollar
- "Anxious for Nothing: Finding Calm in a Chaotic World" by Max Lucado

www.ingramcontent.com/pod-product-compliance
Lightning Source LLC
LaVergne TN
LVHW041153150826
845673LV00001B/144

9798227826282